RELIGIOUS EDUCATION AND THE BRAIN

A Practical Resource for Understanding How We Learn about God

JERRY LARSEN

D1115435

PAULIST PRESS
New York/Mahwah, N.J.

Cover design by Frank Vitale

Library of Congress Cataloging-in-Publication Data

Larsen, Jerry.
    Religious education and the brain : a practical resource for understanding how we learn about God / Jerry Larsen.
        p.   cm.
    Includes bibliographical references.
    ISBN 0-8091-3934-0 (alk. paper)
    1. Religious education—Psychology.   I. Title.

BL42.L37 2000
291.7'5'019—dc21

99-086126

Published by Paulist Press
997 Macarthur Boulevard
Mahwah, New Jersey 07430

www.paulistpress.com

Printed and bound in the
United States of America

Contents

iv   *Contents*

Introduction

IT WAS A TYPICAL Sunday morning at the church where I worked in West Los Angeles. Each morning after adult classes and children's activities, my habit was to make a mad dash from a class to the sanctuary for worship. Without fail there would be a flock of children clogging the hallway waiting to be herded into worship. As usual, I was late. As I waded into the group of kids with urgent warnings about the start of our morning celebrations, my robe sleeve caught the handrail near the door to the front of the sanctuary and it ripped royally as I went sprawling. When I opened my eyes after the fall, I saw a small face with a worried look about three inches from my nose. Its owner said, "You look just like the man in the window so I will be the key."

My friend assumed I understood. I didn't. She struggled to help me up and I walked into the sanctuary with her to the front pew where many of the children sat. I still didn't understand her reference as we sat down waiting for the choir to start. She tugged on the torn part of the robe to get my attention and pointed to one of the high narrow stained-glass windows that depicts the events in the life of Jesus. The sanctuary is a richly visual environment. There are carvings, stained glass, colors and the large open spaces that seem to invite wonder. "See?" she asked, and pointed to one of the windows that is not so easily seen. It was of a figure in a robe reaching up as though for assistance and just above his hand was a large key. She had lived with that image for some time and it meant something to her. It seemed to mean that when you fall there will be something to grab onto: a key to getting up. She was my key that morning.

Over the thirty years I have worked as a Christian educator in a local church, I have become increasingly aware of the central role sight, vision, images and symbols play in the formation of a person's faith and identity. That episode reminded me again. Just consider the range of religious visual expression humanity has generated: the stained glass of European cathedrals, Hindu sculpture, Mormon architecture, Russian Orthodox icons, the monoliths of the Druids and even the cave drawings of Lascaux. They all bear witness to the central place of space and vision in human religious aspiration.

At a personal level, I recall the portraits of Jesus on my grandmother's kitchen walls, the statues of the Way of the Cross at a Roman Catholic retreat center, the pictures produced by children asked to draw God—all these point to the special relationship of sight and image to belief and faith.

1

Thanks to a conversation I had with a friend about an intense religious moment, this mild curiosity about the place of the visual in faith formation turned into a puzzle I had to solve. My friend Francis shared with me a time as a college student when she was struggling with what she believed was a calling to be a journalist. Francis was a deeply religious person. She said that after a long night of prayer and confusion, she seemed to see Jesus next to her. She felt a presence and brightness that filled her up with self-confidence and hope that she was supposed to be a writer. It was a clear picture, she said, and that if she could only see, she would very much like to paint it. Francis was legally blind. She knew quite well that the picture which took shape in her mind was mostly her own inner creation, but it remained with her as an image of God's love and care. Even in her blindness, vision was at work.

Just what is it about images that moves even my blind friend to faithful decisions? Does seeing have some special function in the building of our beliefs?

Early on in my reflection and investigation two ideas began to take shape. First, what one sees, and the images one uses for thinking, shapes one's faith. If I fill my experiences with visions of love and grace, so will my faith be informed. If I see mostly pain and chaos, so will my faith be informed. Second, visual experience and mental images have special power to facilitate the organization of our experiences. Just think of all the religious symbols we use to summarize our theologies.

This connection between seeing and believing has been an especially elusive one. But the power of the visual to ignite imagination and form meaning continued to remind me that something powerful was at the heart of the process.

Several years of study about the place of the visual in the formation of a person's spirit have led me in wider and wider circles of exploration. These circles began to describe a scope of interest that roughly covers the study of *cognition*. Instead of asking how seeing and visualizing relates to one's faith, I found that questions aimed at understanding the way information and experience are organized and processed in the brain were more fruitful. The growing amount of information being generated about the lateralized or "split" nature of the cortex, the discoveries about the way memory is organized, and about cognitive processes in general further opened up my thinking.

My intention, then, is to write of the relationship between our religious life and thought and the way information and ideas are created, stored and retrieved, and to use this knowledge to inform the way we nurture each other's faith.

This book will present nine principles about the way we think and perceive. Special attention will be given to the implications these principles have for education and celebration in congregational life. The nine principles are as follows:

1. It is the nature of the cerebral cortex to make meaning and find patterns from the experiences we accumulate. WE ARE MEANING-MAKERS.
2. Meaning is organized into models of the world against which new data is compared and by which we make our way in the world. OUR MEANINGS MODEL THE WORLD.
3. The way we organized our experiences is heavily influenced by our memories and the "rules of perception." OUR BRAINS EXPERIENCE THINGS THEIR OWN WAY.
4. One of the most important tools in the creation of models and meaning is the ability (even compulsion) to use analogies and metaphors in our thinking. WE LIKE TO KNOW WHAT SOMETHING IS LIKE.
5. What we hold in our memory is organized in a hierarchical network of scripts, stories, stereotypes, and processes. It is stored in a form more basic than either words or pictures. OUR MEMORIES ARE DESIGNED FOR EASY AND QUICK ACCESS.
6. Effective learning of information and skills is a matter of linking that which is to be learned with what we already know. WE NATURALLY TRY TO INTEGRATE ALL WE LEARN.
7. We make meaning, learn skills and solve problems in two distinct thinking styles, using seven intellectual excellencies. EACH PERSON THINKS IN UNIQUE WAYS.
8. Any body of knowledge a person is expected to know includes both knowledge of information and knowledge of skills. The ways by which these two kinds of knowledge are learned are not the same. TEACHING METHODS NEED TO FIT THE KNOWLEDGE BEING TAUGHT.
9. When these principles are at work in a person, one of the most mysterious and powerful results is consciousness. CONSCIOUSNESS IS A RESULT OF BRAIN PROCESSES AND CAN BE NURTURED.

These nine principles are the result of the work of philosophers, cognitive scientists, and educators going back to the time of Socrates. The last fifty years, however, have seen an explosion of information about how we think and believe. What has emerged is a new model of the brain.

My purpose is to describe this new model and apply it to the ways we do religious education. I will offer strategies for using these insights in education and celebrations in congregational life, and to make a case for the need of a holistic approach to religious education and spiritual formation.

The way we go about teaching faith and some of the ways that we celebrate our faith are sadly lacking in power and relevance. Many of our methods are based on incomplete and even wrong ideas about the way we think. We rely too heavily on words. It is time to break the preference for verbal-rational strategies in educational ministry and to forge a new strategy.

CHAPTER ONE

The Lessons of the Brain

JACOB'S ARRIVAL

JACOB, OUR THIRD CHILD, was delivered by Caesarian Section. The doctors allowed me to be with my wife, Linda, to witness the delivery. The memories are still sharp years later. I remember the fear and attraction as the surgeon made the first cuts into Linda—who was wide awake! I recall the smells and sounds of the place. I recall that the doctors talked about their financial investments and families as they opened her up. My eyes were glued to the scalpels and spreaders when up popped a tiny foot! Seeing this little person lifted out of my partner had the effect of putting other events into a perspective that made them seem trivial.

Jacob's birth was at that moment the most vivid and yet unreal experience of my life. My mind still does not have it fully integrated into the assumptions I make about living. When I try to appreciate the sensations and shock that Jacob's system was enduring, I can only wonder. Did he feel it all? Was he aware of the significance of this passage? Was he aware of anything at all? Did it hurt? Did he make any sense of the information that flooded his senses? Will he remember any of it?

The difference between what was happening to Linda and me in that moment of birth and what was happening to Jacob is immense. There is a great dissimilarity between a human who has a history and the human who has but the urge to make one. For his first history-making experience, Jacob was thrust across the gulf into separate humanity. His Pilgrimage had begun.

The trek that begins at birth is to a large degree a journey made possible by the brain and by the brain's systems as they are immersed into a family and culture. What could knowledge of those systems tell us about how to nurture pilgrims? Might knowledge of the brain inform us in religious education? Could it tell us something about the religious educator's agenda and methods? Like a good gardener learning to care for a plant by studying agronomy, wouldn't we be wise to let cognitive science inform religious education? Yes! I propose that the central nervous system can teach us to nurture faith. And not only that, but that our study of how we think and believe will inform our faiths. For me the fundamental revelation is this: that all we are—our personalities, our beliefs, even our very spirits—take shape first in the concert of chemicals, synapses and systems of the tissues of the brain. In a literal way, spirit is born of the flesh.

LESSON NUMBER ONE:
THE NEW BRAIN HAS A FULL AGENDA

The moment of birth is more like the graduation of a student than a cold start of an engine. The day of our birth marked that moment when we separate from the matrix of the womb. It was within that matrix that the essentials of separate life were formed. The months of development before birth were full of landmark events, not the least of which had to do with the development of nerve tissue. It is testimony to the importance of the brain that the greater amount of oxygen and food supplied to the fetus is directed to the formation of nerve tissue. The nearly nine months of development in mother might best be described as nine months of neurological development that just happens to be accompanied by the development of the rest of the body and its systems.[1]

Consider this: In just 18 days after conception, the first neural cells appear, marking the rapid and intricate development of the brain. The brain and spinal cord change from hints of a nervous system to a sort of stalk with a bulb at one end. Within weeks it achieves the shape and segmentation that we are familiar with. By the time the baby arrives, the brain and its related sensors have been at work for weeks. The genetic plan has already "etched" into the circuitry of the infant brain programs that make the baby human able to take *on* and take *in* the world that buzzes around it.

Mammals come in two varieties: cocial and precocial. Cocial mammals are the ones that are mostly complete at birth. Thus, animals like the horse or cow are able to find their "land legs" within hours after leaving their amniotic "ocean." They begin to explore their worlds within a day or two. Precocial mammals, on the other hand, are those mammals who, when born, cannot thrive without the nearly constant attention of the mother and/or father. Precocials still have a good bit of development and growth that must take place before they are "complete."[2]

Humans are precocial. We are born with an incomplete respiratory system, skeletal system, muscular system, digestive system, and most importantly with a partially developed nervous system. For us, mother/father will continue to be our matrix for at least two years.

In those two years the brain makes huge strides toward completion. These strides include 1) the multiplying of connections from one brain cell to another (the web of connectors between nerve cells called dendrites) as learning and stimulation happens; 2) the completion of the bundles of nerves that connect the left and right cortex; 3) the full insulation of the billions of neurons with tissue called myelin; 4) the development of cells and cell connections in the frontal lobes that, when completed, allows the person to make plans, remember instructions and restrain what he or she learns is inappropriate behavior.[3]

Yes, horses do get their acts together faster than we do, but our acts are considerably more complex and a larger part of our behavior has to be learned. Still, we are born with a few tricks tucked away in the tissues of our brains. When Jacob arrived, many of his programs showed themselves right away. His arms flew out when he was turned or put down quickly (the "moro reflex" that restores balance), he was able to hold someone's finger (the grasping reflex), he pushed his head against Linda's neck when his face was caressed (the rooting reflex), he sneezed when the doctor shined a light into his closed eyes (sneezing reflex), and his mouth greeted the world with the sucking response.[4]

Many of these inborn programs insure the child's safety. For example, infants are born with the ability to recognize a "cliff edge" (like the edge of a bed or table) and avoid the drop-off, even if they have never before experienced a dangerous "cliff." The presence of this "hard-wired" depth perception has been demonstrated in experiments where babies were placed on a half-transparent, half-opaque table. The babies could not venture onto the transparent part that seemed to be the edge of the table even when coaxed by their mothers. The babies innately perceived the "cliff" and reacted to it as if were a danger.[5]

Other inborn programs aid vision. They are the strategies of scanning and pursuit. Seeing anything is a complex process. There are numerous points at which the process can be interrupted, including the very pointing of the eyes at an object of interest. There are three actions that the muscles of the eyes have to perform if there is to be seeing: rapid or jerking movements (saccades) from shape to shape, the smooth pursuit motion after a shape is attended to, and the rapid, minute tremor that keeps the image from going "stale" on a particular part of the retina. (It seems that if an image continues to fall on exactly the same cells of the retina, the cells would become desensitized and the image would fade.) The saccadic motion is the search strategy that allows the baby to scan the world for shapes and shades, and for things of interest and meaning. The pursuit or "locking on" ability makes it possible for the baby to watch long enough to satisfy her interest.[6]

We are born with programs that aid social interaction. Many researchers believe we are born with a program that leads a baby to look for and "recognize" a face. With the aid of eye tracking equipment, researchers are able to trace the movement of a baby's eyes as it scans pictures of faces. There is an unmistakable triangular scanning pattern that, when superimposed on the picture, traces the lines between eyes and mouth. This behavior is already in place at birth. Of all the objects that a baby could scan, faces (and even pictures of faces) are nearly always preferred. Facial recognition is "hardwired."[7]

Some of these "interaction" programs involve both the baby and mother. Crying, smiling, rooting, nursing and grasping are programs present at the child's beginning. Together they work to create a bond between the mother and baby. This bond becomes the anchor for the baby's life. The bond and empathetic give-and-take between the mother and baby is even generalized to the degree that babies only a few weeks old are able to empathize with other "faces" in their worlds. Their vital signs resonate naturally with the joy and distress of other babies as well as with their mothers.[8]

Perhaps the most surprising of the inborn programs for social action is the ability to use words. Dr. Noam Chomsky's pioneering work in language development points to the conclusion that, although we are not born with language, we seem to be born with a set of programs that acts as a set of rules for grammar and syntax.[9] As Chomsky studied the way children of many diverse cultures learn language he found similarities in the syntax mistakes children made from culture to culture. These "mistakes," he concluded, were evidence of inborn rules of grammar and syntax. Some of these "natural" rules have to be "unlearned" in order to conform with the child's native language. Chomsky is convinced that grammar and syntax are inborn. At the very least, the fascination for and attention to talking is a given for an infant. However meaningless the words and sounds, what parent has not "conversed" with his or her newborn with the rapt attention and even vocal response being contributed by the infant? These operations and "rules," Chomsky would argue, are made possible by our genetic code.[10]

The point is, babies are not "blank slates." What is etched on the genetic slate at birth are programs and reflexes making each newborn poised to "consume" the world, to seek out patterns in it, to commune and communicate, to recreate the secure duet it left at birth, to organize its experiences and to survive. Every child is busy recreating the world it experiences—a world of *meaning*.

Our first lesson is this: A person, although physically incomplete at birth, does not begin life without an agenda and *modus operandi*. Rather, a person shows up looking for faces, ready to eat, able to alert parents of trouble, cautious of its space, and hungry—voraciously hungry—for patterns of experience that can be made sense of. The new brain is not so much a sponge soaking up whatever washes over it. It is rather like a very hungry wolf looking for food in a domain it has never stalked before. Its food is meaning.

This lesson means that religious educators don't have to train people to be philosophers, theologians and pilgrims; that is what we are. We are not called to *make* people religious or to attract them to things of the spirit; we are called to gather the resources of our traditions and present them as tools for the spirit journeys each one has been on since birth.

LESSON TWO:
THE BRAIN CREATES THE WORLD

However incomplete, the new human embarks immediately on the hunt for meaning and pattern. In concert with its needs for food, warmth, and touching, the new person begins to take in the world in patterns. Eyes, ears, nose, tongue and skin are not as discerning as they will become, but they are sensitive to those things that are necessary to be comfortable and to feel pleasure. Through them, the baby's brain goes about its task of building a model of the world that he or she begins to depend upon. Ideally, at the center of the child's world will be a model built out of the warmth of skin, soft sounds, and the pleasant taste and scent that it will later know as parent.

As eyes and ears begin to collect information, the child's world widens and becomes deeper. With the help of "pre-wired" strategies, the child is able to enjoy and even exert some control over the world. Faces (human and animal) begin to stand out as distinct submodels that live in his or her world. The first year is a sort of reprise of the cosmic "big bang," except that it happens in the head of this new human rather than at the center of the universe. It is an explosion of patterns and meaning within the mind of the child. The child comes into the world with no preconceptions or expectations of what this place is. The template is blank, but with the help of the strategies for grasping patterns, the model begins to take shape immediately.[11]

Why must we depend on the models of self, home, family, yard, street, and so on? Why is it not possible to simply take each new experience as it comes and act within it as the raw data demands? The answer lies at the heart of the way we think. Action grows out of understanding. We can't act meaningfully in a situation unless we have some degree of understanding of it. Understanding happens when what we experience matches memories that we have already arranged into a meaningful pattern. This "template matching," as cognitive scientists call it, makes recognition possible and at the same time is the procedure whereby our attention gets focused.[12]

Let me use Jacob as an example of the way the modeling makes it possible to recognize things and to focus attention. Jacob shared a room with his older brother Nathan. He became "at home" with the room as a model of it took shape in his brain. It was familiar. Not long after Jacob started living in the room, Linda added animal pictures at eye level near his crib. Most of the pictures showed the faces of the animals quite clearly. When he saw them for the first time, his attention was drawn to them. He was drawn first because his model did not include these pictures as part of the room. His template of the room did not include what he saw on the wall. This mismatch drew his eyes to the novelty of the pictures. His attention was held because the pictures scored a match with another model in his active brain: faces. Any change of the environment would have caused Jacob's attention to become focused on the change for a moment just because of the mismatch between expectation and experience. Jacob gazed for a long while (long for a baby) at the pictures. He was drawn to something novel and was surprised to recognize something pleasantly familiar. He spent several moments going from one picture to the other, touching the eyes of the animals and making sounds babies make when they interact with their world happily.

For the rest of Jacob's life, it will be the unfolding, evolving, and sometimes drastically reconstructed models of life that will make it possible for him to act and be in the world. So important is this modeling that Jacob (like you or me) will hold on to old models and beliefs long after he gets new and contradictory information. Similarly he will, when an important situation or experience seems baffling, make mighty leaps of logic and jumps to conclusion on the slimmest of evidence just to be able to quench the nagging need to make sense of things.

So what does that mean for our task as religious educators? It means that all the data, skills, information and concepts that make up religious curriculum are of value to the pilgrim only to the degree they contribute to a meaningful model of the world. It means that our success at teaching will be revealed more by testing a student's models than by testing a student's mastery of data and skills. Yet, it also means that the steps to building high fidelity models of life must include mastery of new skills and information. Finally, it means that our role as educators is primarily one of guide, witness or docent. This way of teaching trusts the student to take what is experienced and make his or her *own* sense of the world.

LESSON THREE:
THE MULTIPLEX BRAIN

In the late seventies at UCLA, methods were developed whereby a camera was able to photograph cross sections of a human brain sequentially from base to top. Each cross section was just a fraction of a centimeter thick so that there were hundreds of "slices" photographed before a brain was completely mapped. When shown as a movie at 16 frames per second, the viewer is able to visually "glide" through the physical structures of the brain. When I first saw the film, I experienced the same kind of perception that I did on my first viewing of a photograph of the Earth from space. As the Earth picture was able to fill out my model of Earth-in-space, so the brain movie was able to offer a clearer perspective of the brain-in-the-head. The readjustment was so complete as to make it possible for me to imagine the brain in a new way and with far more clarity and wholeness than before.

I want to offer a verbal tour of the structures of the brain emerging out of that insight. It won't have the impact of the motion picture tour, but I hope it will reveal to you the multiplex nature of the brain: the variety of ways the brain receives, processes and organizes information and experiences. The more we understand its extensive repertoire of strategies, the better we can craft events and experiences that will help persons build their worlds and faith.

BOTTOM-TO-TOP:
WHERE WE THINK (See Figure 1.1)

When the brain is described from the base to the top, there emerges a unique pattern. Briefly, the pattern is this: the structures are arranged as a sort of analog of the evolution of vertebrate brains. The first vertebrates (fish, reptiles and birds) required very specific central nervous system functions that

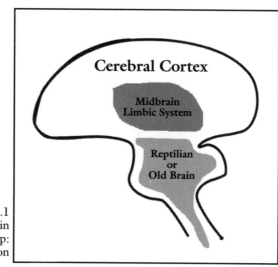

Figure 1.1
The Human Brain
From Bottom to Top:
A History Lesson

could control the relative complexity of their bodies. They needed a complex memory system, a complex regulatory system and a new attention system for dealing with feeding and with predators. Our brains contain the same structures. They are clustered about the brain stem and are sometimes called the reptilian brain or the old brain. The first of these structures is the cerebellum. It is a baseball-size structure that is our "automatic pilot." When Jacob was learning to walk, he had to perform a deliberate and considered set of actions. As his muscles became more responsive to his intentions, the set of operations that he had to perform became automatic. Now he runs, jumps, and walks without a thought about the complicated concert of motions that are required. In fact, if he had to think of all the steps needed to run he would not be able to do it. The motions are now orchestrated and timed by the cerebellum—automatically. Every vertebrate animal has a well-developed cerebellum or its like.[13]

If the cerebellum is the automatic pilot, the ascending reticular system is the alarm and the regulatory system. Like a shaft buried up into the brain, the reticular system is made up of the Medulla Oblongata (regulates essential functions like breathing), the Reticular Formation (regulates sleep and wakefulness and is responsible for arousing the attention of the cortex), and the Pons (also responsible for awareness and attention).[14]

Located at the top of the pons and around it like a mushroom are the structures known as the midbrain or the Limbic System. The midbrain includes the Thalamus (responsible for routing impulses from the old brain and the midbrain to the cortex as well as for the generation of emotions), the Hypothalamus (responsible for sending signals of hunger, thirst and sexual arousal to the cortex), the Hippocampus (responsible for linking new experience and insights with pleasure and for differentiating very close sequences of experience into serial events that the cortex can decode into meaning—as in reading or listening to a person's words), and several other tiny structures having to do with emotions, smell and the integration of the various structures. The Limbic System is the source of our emotions, pleasure and pain, and spurs the cortex to action with help from the pons.[15]

Finally at the top of the brain, like a cap protecting the more primitive structures, is the cerebral cortex. Whereas the old and midbrains have very definite functions for each structure, the cortex is the "generalist" member of the brain "team." It is responsible for functions like memory storage, planning, meaning-making, calculation, speech, voluntary muscle control and consciousness. Many of these functions are not located in specific places. In fact, some seem to be spread out all over the cortex. It is the most massive of all the structures of the brain and is the latest development in animal evolution.

So, as we scan the brain from bottom to top, what is revealed is a living chronicle of brain evolution. At the base, automatic regulatory functions grind on from moment to moment. In the midbrain the mechanisms for attention, arousal and emotions find their origins. Then in the cortex, memory and moment combine with feeling and attention to generate meaning, thoughts, voluntary action and self-awareness.[16] Where we think is at the top—the cortex. But it depends on the functioning of the older structures.

BACK-TO-FRONT:
WHAT WE THINK (See Figure 1.2)

As the bottom-to-top scan tells us something about the natural history of the brain, the back-to-front scan can tell us something of the vastness and range of functions that find their origins in the cortex. This is not to say that one can locate all these functions in precise positions (although some can be located); rather it is to say that there are general areas of the cortex that are dedicated to more-or-less specific functions. As we consider these areas from back-to-front we will gain a sense of the cortex's enormous work and general "division of labor."[17]

The cortex is grayish in color, divided into two halves or hemispheres, and is convoluted into folds. Yet it looks uniform. Let's begin at the back of the brain and move forward with an eye toward discovering some of the functions that are more or less localized. The very back of the cortex is that area called the Occipital Lobe. This palm-sized area is the receiver of nerve signals from the eyes. It is responsible for decoding visual information into

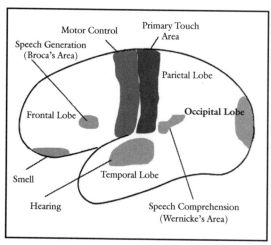

Figure 1.2
The Human Brain
From Back To Front:
What We Think

patterns that can be compared to visual memories and models already in the brain. If there is any part of the cortex that has a special look that sets it apart from the rest of the cortex, it is this area. The occipital lobes (or "striate" or "visual" cortex, as the area is sometimes called) are actually a magnified "map" of the eyes' retinas. The cell arrangement of this area is such that it looks striped and the cells receive data from a corresponding area of either the right or left half or the retina of each eye.[18]

The largest sections of the cortex are the Parietal Lobes occupying roughly the middle top and sides of the cortex. They include the areas that deal with touch, language (on the left side more so than on the right), motor control, and other of the senses. However, most of the cells of the Parietal lobes are "uncommitted." That is to say that there is no specific action, perception or cognition that is controlled by the uncommitted region.

Below the parietal regions on either side of the brain are large folds called the Temporal Lobes. These lobes are concerned with the interpreting of signals from the inner ears: They contribute to our sense of scale when we perceive objects visually, and there is some involvement of the temporal region in "tagging" memories with the emotional tone that we might call "familiarity." This latter conclusion is supported by experiences of persons who suffer from epilepsy originating from a temporal lobe. It seems that when the emotional tone is recalled by itself, it causes what is popularly known as déjà vu. The tone comes to consciousness along with the sense that whatever one is presently experiencing is familiar. We all have those experiences. Temporal lobe epileptics are flooded with this déjà vu feeling during a seizure.[19] Beyond these functions, the cells of the temporal lopes are also uncommitted.

The two Frontal Lobes are highly developed in human beings. Other primates have them, but they are not as prominent as they are in humans. Although they too contain large areas of uncommitted neurons, there are three specific functions that operate there. One is to serve as the decoding place of signals from the olfactory nerves that allow us to perceive smells.

The second function of the frontal lobes has to do with planning. From this front part of the brain originates the mechanism for keeping our attention on a plan that we devise. When we set a plan in motion, its success depends on our keeping our minds on the end goal as well as keeping the steps in our consciousness. This is accomplished by a peculiar brain wave frequency that is generated in the front of our heads. It is called the expectancy wave (the Contingent Negative Variation or CNV wave) and is a sort of "place keeper" as we plan. If you have ever become distracted from what you were working on and forgotten a task in progress, you may have experienced a nagging feeling that there was something that you forgot or left unfinished.

That feeling is a product of the CNV wave pulling you back to the unfinished task.[20]

The third function located in the frontal lobes has to do with inhibitions and social restraint. Taboos, mores, and social convention are enforced from the front of the brain. Perhaps the most dramatic evidence of this connection between the frontal cortex and social restraint comes to us from the unfortunate experience of Phineas Gage. Mr. Gage was a Vermont railroad foreman who, in 1848, was struck in the head by a metal rod as a result of an explosion. The rod went clean through his forehead and left frontal lobe. Gage survived without any impairment to his overall health or intellect. But as a result, kindly, patient, hard-working, soft-spoken Phineas Gage became, for the rest of his life, "fitful, irreverent, indulging at times in the grossest profanity . . . manifesting but little deference to his fellows, impatient of restraint or advice when it conflicts with his desires" (as quoted from his physician). When Gage died, an autopsy revealed extensive damage to the front portion of his left frontal lobe. He was described as childlike in his attention span and awareness of the social consequences of his actions. Childlike is an apt description because the frontal lobe nerve pathways are not fully developed in humans until perhaps 15 or 16 years of age.[21]

This back-to-front look at the cortex leads me to two perceptions. The first is that the cortex has a lot to do. It is not that the tasks are so varied, rather it is that the overall job that the tasks contribute to is so large. By receiving and assimilating the constant input from the senses, the cortex is fired up by the older parts of the brain to remake the outside world on the inside—not just the physical world, but the ecology of social and human interconnection of which it is a part. It is an impossible job, yet here we are!

The second perception is that the cortex has to be flexible and efficient enough to always be "making up its mind." Thus the millions of uncommitted neurons wait to be programmed and reprogrammed with memory, skills, plans, perceptions, cognitive processes and awareness. While there is an impressive difference between the other mammals and humans as to the size of the brain, the more impressive difference is in the amount of uncommitted cerebral cortex. Our "gray matter" is a vast storehouse and processing plant for our perceptions of the entire universe!

LEFT-TO-RIGHT:
HOW WE THINK (See Figure 1.3)

The third axis that can be meaningfully traveled is the one that explores the cortex from left to right. The back-to-front look reveals to us various places

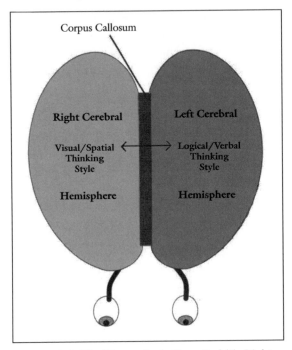

Figure 1.3 The Human Brain From Left To Right:
How We Think

that the cortex uses to arrange and model the physical and social world. The left-to-right look shows us a range of thinking styles that we employ in order to understand and add to the world.

The left and right halves of the cortex are, on the surface, roughly mirror images of each other. There is some evidence that one tends to be larger than the other, but the data indicates that it is a matter of individual diversity. The two halves or cerebral hemispheres are connected by a thick "cable" of 200 million nerve fibers called the corpus callosum.[22] At birth this connector is relatively small and does not function to the capacity that it does in adulthood. At some time during adolescence, the connector reaches its mature size and function. It is through this connector that most of the information and cognitive abilities of the two sides are integrated.

Nothing in our physical makeup is without function, and that is especially true of the brain. What are the functions of the two-sided nature of the cortex? First, its lateralized nature means that the spatial sensations (touch, sight, hearing, and to a degree smell) are registered in the cortex spatially. The left brain receives the impulses that represent the right side of the world and the right brain receives the ones for the left side of the world. Likewise, the lateralized nature of the cortex means that the voluntary muscles of the body that are mirrored on each side are instructed from one side of the cortex's motor control or the other. The left side of the body is instructed by the right motor area and the right side of the body is instructed by the left motor area of the cortex.[23]

But there is more. There are some functions that are controlled from one side only, without any mirrored control on the other. Language is the clearest case in point (refer to illustration 1.2). Since Paul Broca first documented, around 1860, the relation of brain damage to the loss of speech, it has been more or less taken for granted that speaking and understanding words are functions that are controlled (in most people) from specific areas of the left cortex. In fact there are two areas that are now known to control language functions: Broca's Area,[24] located just above the left temple (it controls the ability to form spoken words), and Wernicke's Area,[25] located above and behind the left ear (it controls the ability to understand words). When there is injury to any of these areas, there is language loss of some kind. There is no corresponding area on the right side.

What is found when there is damage (due to accident or stroke) to the right cortex is that spatial perception is most often affected. Victims of this sort of damage are many times left without any awareness of one whole side of their world, or they are no longer able to find their way from one place to another.

One of the puzzles of the asymmetry of the cortex is that some of the functions that are lateralized in adults seem not to be lateralized in children. Language is again the prime example. Medical research into cases where there has been brain damage to the speech centers of adults usually show little return of full speech. Yet similar damage to children does not mean loss of speech anywhere near the rate it does in adults. The younger the child, the better the recovery. The conclusion is that speech and language in young children is still not permanently located on one side or the other. If there is damage to what is becoming the speech center, the uncommitted cortex is new and vast enough to take up the slack. In adults, the cortex is not so pliable or unused.

The asymmetrical nature of what the cortex does has spawned a great deal of research, debate and conjecture. When it is sorted out, what is firm is that the left cortex is the verbal/logical brain and the right cortex is the visio/spatial brain. Not only does this mean that the left brain controls speech and language understanding and the right handles visual and spatial data, it also means that the way that memories and data are processed by the left tends to be verbal and sequential and that the right tends to use images and be more holistic. The thinking styles of the left and right are different.

Just how they are different is hard for scientists to pin down but a composite list of left-right thinking style descriptions looks like this:

LEFT	RIGHT
logical	intuitive
intellectual	sensual
rational	mythical
abstract	concrete
sequential	holistic
verbal	visual/spatial
scientific	poetic[26]

There seems to be two ways of processing information corresponding to the two hemispheres, but within the two hemispheres there is even more division of labor. Evaluating human cognitive abilities just in terms of left-right thinking skills is a bit too simple. The split-brain research has led to discoveries about intelligence in general and the discovery that we have at least seven distinct cognitive abilities. Asymmetry studies paved the way to this broadened view of intelligence. We will look at this fresh approach in a later chapter.

THEME AND VARIATION

My intention has been to give the reader a glimpse of the "equipment" of the brain and of some of its essential programs with which we are born. I have tried to show that these programs and the organization of the brain make us beings that seek pattern and meaning in our experience. Further, we create models of the world in our brains that allow us to interact with the world and to be creative within it. This is the "theme" around which each of us composes unique variations. Jacob was born "itching" to find and create patterns within a meaningful world. From here on out his models and creations will be similar to others but still one-of-a-kind in a world full of one-of-a-kinds. How fulfilled and creative his pilgrimage will be will depend on many factors, but at the base three cognitive variables will be at work:

1) his ability to use both his verbal/logical and his visio/spatial thinking styles and their related functions, intelligences and programs;
2) his ability to acquire, use and reorganize his stock of knowledge and memories that are "high fidelity" models of the world as it is; and
3) his ability to be a self-aware agent within his world.

It is from these three abilities that a person can engage and contribute to a world.

In the religious communities we are concerned with the pilgrimages of persons. Each person walks the same ageless path toward meaning but with a unique stride. It is our vocation to help in the equipping of pilgrims. What would we conclude if we test the content and methods of education and nurture in our congregations? Would we find it strong or weak from this cognitive perspective? Would we find that we are encouraging fresh variations on the human theme, or would we find that we are trying to teach only one song? Would we find that we are encouraging religious thinking and acting that is mostly verbal or visual? Would we find persons being encouraged to be creators and pilgrims all their lives or simply for the first eighteen years? Would we find that the methods we use for education are a pleasure or a bore? Would we find a richness of history and tradition that adds to a person's usable stock of knowledge and self-awareness, or would the history and tradition be scattered around as stumbling blocks for seekers? Would we find teachers that are respectful guides or controlling keepers of secrets?

I have no doubt that the brain works in such a way that human beings cannot help but be religious. We are biologically moved to seek faith and live in fidelity with our visions—our models—of the universe. If that drive is propelled by the motor we call the brain, then religious educators and leaders must look closely at how it works. Not only will we be informed in the way we nurture faith, but we may also see the imprint of that which makes life and meaning possible.

CHAPTER TWO

The Meaning Factory

QUILTERS

EARLY IN 1985 Linda and I went to the Los Angeles Music Center to see the play *Quilters*. The play is a frontier family history told from the perspective of women pioneers. It captures the ordeal of three generations of women and their families as they settled in the Midwest. The quilts the women created served to link together the episodes of the play. These women used quilts to tell their stories, maintain their self-respect and hold on to a vision of hope. The quilts (crafted especially for the play after designs by settler women of the last century) were models of the minds and spirits of the women sewn together in a way that captured their integrity and dreams. At the conclusion of the play, as the main character recalled her life story, a giant quilt-of-quilts was lifted high over her head. It was moving to see the symbols and metaphors of this woman's life stretch some 25 feet high and wide behind her. Her "heritage quilt" and her life were celebrated.

The quilts and the play provided a fresh understanding of how natural and crucial it is that we make sense of our lives. For those quilters, to quilt was an affirmation of faith growing out of the visions, aspirations, events, and struggles of the quilter. To make a quilt was not just a way to pass time or manufacture a necessity. It was an opportunity to make a witness and pass on a tradition. For them, the quilt was a product of one's spirit—a representation of the core of one's life.

QUILT FACTORIES

Like patches for a quilt, our memories wait to be attached to themes and motifs we claim as our own. Think of the quilt itself as the patchwork of ways human beings give expression to what is held in memory. Our brains are the factories producing those expressions. They are like factories in four ways (see Figures 2.1A and 2.1B). First, just as factories function only to the degree that there are raw materials in a warehouse, so our brains require a "warehouse" of memory that can be fashioned into meaningful expressions.

Second, as a factory uses methods, machinery and processes to combine the elements of the warehouse, so the brain is equipped with its own "manufacturing" systems that combine memories and thoughts into meaningful expression and action.

Third, just as a factory has a shipping and receiving department that readies its products for shipment and receives materials that it needs for the creation of the product, so the brain has a two-way "shipping and receiving" system called "working memory" and "consciousness." In working memory, meaningful expressions *to* the world are prepared and it is the work space for examining data *from* the world.

Finally, as the factory has a loading dock where shipments can be received, so the brain has the "loading dock" of the senses where data is momentarily held, allowing the brain to begin processing it.

I don't mean to trivialize the processes of thought with the factory analogy. Rather, I hope that the image will communicate something of the integrity of the thinking processes. The brain and its work have often been

Figure 2.1A

B = SHIPPING AND RECEIVING

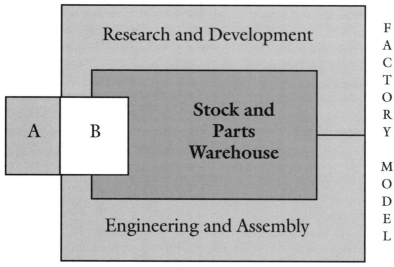

A = LOADING DOCK

Figure 2.1B

B = SHORT-TERM MEMORY

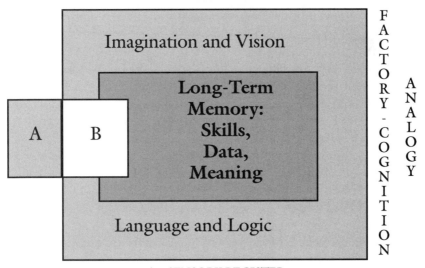

A = SENSORY REGISTER

described using metaphors: from black box to computer, and from blank slate to the branches of government. I choose the factory metaphor because it is a familiar system to most people and because it cannot be mistaken for the brain itself. Too often an analogy becomes so identified with the thing that it tries to illuminate that it ceases to be thought of as an analogy but is thought of as a description. The comparison of computer to brain can lead to such a mistake.

THE MEANING FACTORY AT WORK:
GOING TO THE CIRCUS

Consider the analogy between factory and brain in more detail. The "floor plan" of the meaning factory is represented by Figure 2.1C. It is "littered" with resources, subsystems, processes and routines. As the human brain has evolved, it has accumulated hundreds of ways of making sense of experience. My diagram is meant to give the impression of a meaning factory crammed with ways to deal with the raw material of the world, and yet my cluttered sketch only hints at the complexity of what goes on in our heads.

Perhaps a personal experience—attending Ringling Brothers, Barnum

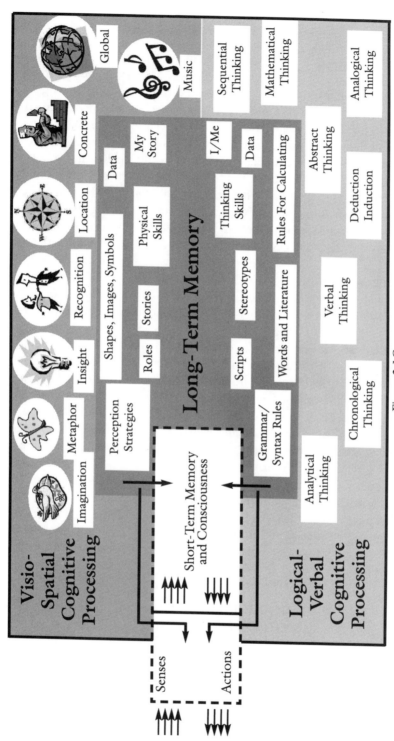

Figure 2.1C
The Brain as Meaning Factory:
The Factory "Floor Plan"

and Bailey Circus—can serve as an example of the factory of meaning at work. Linda and I decided to take the kids to the circus. Finally the day arrived. That afternoon we drove to the Forum and took the long walk across the parking lot to the arena. I remember feeling a bit disappointed as we arrived but I didn't really know why. As we entered the Forum, sounds, smells and sights began to change my mood as the Circus began to impress itself on me. There were animal and cotton candy smells, the sounds of hawkers, and down at the far end of the stadium, the pandemonium of the circus band tuning up. Maybe the seats weren't the best, but there were three rings down on the floor of the arena, clowns wandering about and the peanut sellers already walking the stands. It was becoming a circus to me.

Then with the "TA DA" of the band and the "Ladies and Gentlemen, boys and girls . . ." of the ringmaster, the uneasiness and irritability evaporated: the place was indeed the Circus. I'm sure that I bothered my son Nathan with incessant explanations of what was going on in the place, but he didn't complain and he helped me to live the past and present at once. The rest of the time was simply a nostalgia overdose that was a blur of experience and memory mixed wonderfully in my mind.

Memories seemed to pop out into my awareness at the slightest provocation. A clown would begin a routine with his dog and the whole skit would come to mind instantly. A vendor passed and the smell of peanuts brought back memories of my first midway and sideshow. It was as though the experience was doing to my memories and expectations what a magnet does to iron filings: the circus drew out those memories and rearranged them into a fresh but very familiar pattern.

When it was over, I was aware of a general feeling and impression of the two-and-a-half-hours I spent with my family at the circus. The experience was a whole thing born of a collage of images and feelings. Further, the thing that it was had me in it. It wasn't just CIRCUS. It was MY circus. It could not exist without me. This awareness was strong enough to accompany me to the car. Once homeward bound it faded as the task of driving took center ring.

THE CIRCUS EXPERIENCE
AS THE FACTORY AT WORK

Our brains at rest (or as close as they can come to being at rest) are just itching to produce. They are stocked with memories, skills, knowledge, stereotypes, concepts and data that can be joined and rejoined with the present to create an experience. Such was the case at the circus. Residing within my brain are the past experiences of the circus left there when I was a boy. They include memories of the acts, the clowns, the animals, people, music, and the tent, as well as the feelings I had when I saw Clyde Beatty face wild cats, and the sadness I felt when I saw Emmett Kelly's loneliness. Also included in my memories are the wonder at the tent's size and the fear when I thought I was lost in the crowd.

From the time we set out to attend the circus there was a steady stream of input delivered to my awareness. The fresh experience was already hooking and reeling in the concept of "circus" that resided in the warehouse of my memory. It was that complex of images, roles, stereotypes, stories, and data that took shape as "circus." What happened when I drew near the Forum was a developing uneasiness brought on by the fact that the circus of my memory was not fully realized this time with my eyes (no sideshows! no sawdust! NO TENT!).

Inside the Forum, the reality began to fit my memorized circus and with each new act down in the rings the satisfaction and confirmation overshadowed the disappointment. With the unfolding of the circus events more memories were hooked and brought into my awareness. The hooks that snagged my memories were the sights (colors, shapes, movements, symbols), sounds (the band, the ringmaster's words, the trumpeting of the elephants), smells (popcorn, animals, hot dogs), tastes (cotton candy, Coca Cola), and things touched (the person behind me, the touch of my wife and son, the food and seats).

My memories were able to be hooked and brought to awareness because of the work of the parts of my brain that turn experience into meaning. I was able to make my way in and around the arena to the snack bar because of the spatial thinking happening in the right side of my cortex.[1] I was able to comprehend the meaning of the costume motif of the aerialists because of the metaphorical thinking that goes on in the right. I was able to make sense out of the words of the ringmaster because of the stock of verbal memory and verbal thinking of my left cortex.[2] The meaning of the clown acts depended on spatial thinking (to comprehend the irony of physical humor), visual recognition (to recognize the stereotypical costumes and props), sequential thinking (to sense the story line of their skit), and musical thinking (to understand the musical metaphors that the band added to the skits). In other words, the wedding of memory and experience required not only the raw materials of memory and sensory input, but also required the logical, musical, verbal, spatial, visual, interpersonal, and introspective thinking processes located in various areas of the left and right cortex.[3] The result was an updated and augmented network of memories that I know to be "circus." What I remember being aware of as I walked to our car was this vivid "remake." It had been "manufactured" from my memory and from the events of the day. The finished product was a whole thing, a model, a gestalt, fresh off the assembly line. It wasn't just a rebuilt memory; it was one that had a different "me" than was in attendance at the old 1954 model of the circus. This experience involved my self-concept and self-image. It wasn't just the circus; this new model was "thirty-six-year-old father-husband, still-a-kid Jerry Larsen at the circus for the first time in twenty-six years." It resides in my brain as a network of memories linked to the central and controlling concept, CIRCUS (see Figure 2.2). This network was a *model* I have of "circusness." I want now to expand this concept of modeling.

THE FACTORY'S PRODUCT:
WORKING MODELS OF THE WORLD

A few years ago my wife was a teacher in a preschool in West Los Angeles. She would share with me the little births of meaning she witnessed in the lives of her children. Her descriptions never failed to impress me with their similarity. Each new spurt of cognitive growth represented the coming together of new experiences forming fresh models in the brains of the students. Whether the birth happened in the mind of a four-year-old troublemaker who finds out that he can *say* that he is angry instead of throwing a toy—or that of a fearful child who begins to feel at home at the school—what was happening was the same: the development of a new expectation of the world and of themselves in it.

The product that issued from their young brains was a model or miniature working replica of something that they had not fully grasped before. When a person learns any new idea, process, or skill, it takes "shape" as a model in the brain.[4]

THE ARRAY OF MODELING

Just what are these models?

Allow me to jump to a different analogy other than "factory." Perhaps the array of modeling that we use and store can be compared to the concentric circles of waves caused by a stone thrown into a pool of water (see Figures 2.3A and 2.3B). The inner circles contain the basic models we employ to identify our physical world. The outer ripples contain models of our "meta" physical world, the world of meanings, values, visions and relationships that do not have edges, shape, texture or smell. This stone-in-the-water metaphor is an invention. It separates human experience in arbitrary ways while asserting a central principle: Our models of the way the world is

Figure 2.2

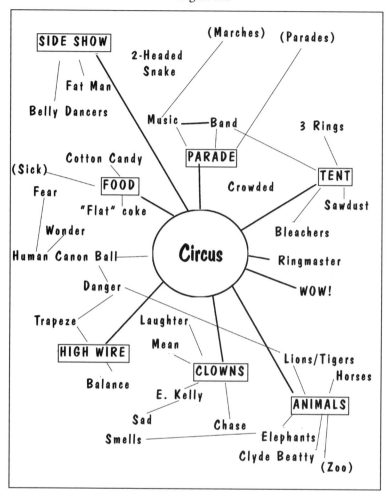

and works starts with sensory experience. From those experiences we build a world of meaning. The ripples caused by experience are not well defined as they propagate outward.

At the center is the stone itself: raw data and experience that we process into patterns according to perception systems that we were born with. The first models we use are the ones that identify the PHYSICAL CHARACTERISTICS of the objects and experience that splash into our pool of meaning (size, mass, color, shading, edges, texture, shape, taste, sound, etc.).

Figure 2.3A
Modeling The World: A Ten-Level Processing System

THE PRIMARY CIRCLES: Making Physical Sense of Experiences

Circle 1. Feature Detection: What our senses receive is first processed at the simplest level identifying shape, color, scent, taste, mass, shading, texture, temperature, etc. These features are recognized when the sensory data is comparing to memories of similar features (e.g., this thing is white, smooth, hard, rounded, tasteless, odorless).

Circle 2. Classification: Once the features of a thing or experience are identified, "the pieces" are combined into a whole and compared to memories of similar things. If there is a "match" between experience and memory, we have identified it as belonging to the similar class of things (e.g., this thing is bowllike, about fist-size with a handle—a cup!

Circle 3. Recognition: When the particular qualities of a thing or experience is grouped with other similar things in a class, it then can be recognized in its particularity (e.g., this is a cup that was a gift from a friend that has a scratch on the side next to the picture of a sunrise—**my** morning cup).

Circle 4. Location: All objects exist in an environment. The final step of physical sense making is to identify the context or background and surroundings of the thing I experience (e.g., this is my cup with hot chocolate on the table in my kitchen at breakfast on a Saturday morning at 7 A.M.

Experience

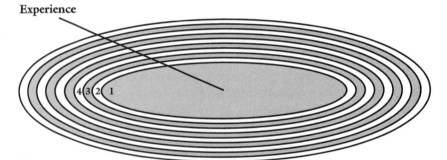

These characteristics are sensed and instantly compared with features we already hold in memory.[5]

The next circle is a quantum leap out ahead of the preliminary feature detection. This second circle contains the models of CLASSES of objects or experiences. At this level we hold models like "cup," "parent," or "joke." As the features of an object/experience are deciphered, our perception systems assigns them into groups or classes. If the features are combined into patterns for which we already have a class-model, then there is a match and we are able to determine that the object is a member of a class of things of which

Figure 2.3B
Modeling The World: A Ten-Level Processing System

THE PRIMARY CIRCLES: Making Meta-physical Sense of Experiences

Circle 5. Identity: In this circle of meaning the model of "me" and "I" takes shape. As I experience the world, act in it, and experience myself as a part of it, I come to have a sense of who I am, of my value and competence, and of my power in my world. This is where I am "invented (I am Jerry, father, husband eating breakfast)."

Circle 6. Community: This circle of meaning includes models of significant human relationships that make up my ecology of spirit. This is the arena where I come to know whose I am and am not, and how I move about in my web of affiliations (as I share breakfast, I am connected to family, friends, and community).

Circle 7. Values: In this circle I manufacture my models of right, wrong, beautiful and ugly. With these models, I can decide right and wrong action and evaluate things aesthetically (it is good to share a meal and enjoy the morning).

Circle 8. Models of history: As we add to our store of experiences over time, we develop a sense of the meaning of the passage of time. We come to believe things about the meaning the past has for the present and of why and how the past is the way it seems to have been. Here is where we create models of history (I am the product of the loving relationships and communities of my history).

Circle 9. Models of the future: Closely related to the meanings of the past are the meanings and beliefs about what will happen next and why. Each of us comes to have models of what will be next and whether what's next will be good or not (if everyone had the experiences of care, love and challenge, our world would be transformed).

Circle 10. Models of the cosmos: The largest ripple of meaning we humans make has to do with what is at the heart of the universe. This circle involves beliefs about how the universe works and evolves, what power or powers animate it and what is ultimately important (the only power in the universe that can redeem human culture is LOVE).

Experience

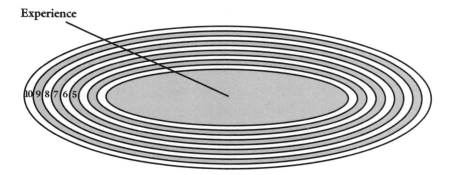

we know. These objects/experiences can be simple (like "mug") or complex (like "circus").[6]

The third circle contains the models of PARTICULAR OBJECTS OR EXPERIENCES like "mug (class) that has my name on it and a chip on the lip," or "my father (class), Howard Larsen." If the object I attend to corresponds to this model, then I recognize what it is I see or hear or touch.

Then encircling these three is the circle of one's models of the world or ENVIRONMENTS wherein the object has a meaningful place. This fourth level of modeling is the one that puts the object into a larger context.

These inner circles of modeling represent the stock of knowledge and models about our physical world.

Let's take **a rock thrown into a pool in a meadow one afternoon** as an example. In our memories there "reside" simple models of edges, corners, weight and color (features). They can be "addressed" in our minds and compared with similar features that our eyes deliver to the striate cortex. Our eyes attend to an object with a certain combination of these features that our brains quickly compare with similar memorized combinations. The comparison scores a "hit" with the memorized class "rock." This rock fits our model of "rock-ness" and can be further classified as a member of one of several kinds of rocks that we have modeled. Finally, we are able to make sense of the context within which we experience the rock as hundreds of other bits of information are similarly analyzed and combined to allow us to identify the "world" the rock is in. The rock-event is identified as "a-rock-in-a-pool-in-a-meadow-one-afternoon" because of the models of the parts and the whole that I have built up and stored over the years. In addition, this particular "rock-in-a-pool-in-a-meadow-one-afternoon" becomes a new experience that will be added to and will modify my old memories.

But there are more radiating circles of meaning that help identify an experience and which an experience effects. The next waves represent the way our brains take the physical conclusions and invent the meta-physical.

I use the term *meta-physical* in a very narrow sense. *Meta* refers to that which is on top of or derived from something more basic. These meanings are not represented in the physical world the way a rock is; rather, they are "on top of" the physical experiences we have; they are what the sensory experiences can *mean*.

The fifth circle contains the system of self perceptions that add up to MODELS OF ONE'S SELF, my identities, my "me," myself-in-the-world.

It includes a history of a growing and evolving self that is connected to me now. It includes models of me failing and succeeding, of me alone and in relationship with individual people and with groups. It is that system of models and memories that British writer Gordon Taylor calls "EGOGE" (ee/go/gee), meaning "I myself."[7] Taylor writes that it is not just ego or personality but rather it is the model I have of myself. It is what Eric Erikson refers to when he describes the coalescing of a person's "identity" during the years of adolescence.

In fact, the model is so rich and complex, it takes fifteen to twenty years for a person to develop and become fully aware of this model of self-in-the-world.[8]

This self or *egoge* that I am conscious of is a system of models that acts like a player in and amongst the models of the world I have built in my mind. It serves to connect events and memories into a narrative of my self-over-time. When I do something, I immediately have a sense of whether it is consistent with the "me" that I have modeled.

During the teenage years the dawning of an awareness of the self is both liberating and frightening. It is as though a haze begins to lift from one's life story to reveal a self. It is a self, however, that is tenuous and easily fogged in or lost.

In J. D. Salinger's *The Catcher in the Rye,* the hero, Holden Caufield, experiences a horror that young people feel when they seem not to have a good grip on a sense of self. In one scene, Holden is trying to get to his sister at the end of a confused and painful weekend. As he walks the streets of New York, the feeling of losing touch with his self becomes overwhelming:

> Anyway, I kept walking and walking up Fifth Avenue, without any tie on or anything. Then all of a sudden, something very spooky started happening. Every time I came to the end of the block and stepped off the goddam curb, I had this feeling that I'd never get to the other side of the street. I thought I'd just go down, down, down, and nobody'd ever see me again. Boy did it scare me. You can't imagine. I started sweating like a bastard— my whole shirt, and underwear, and everything. Then I started doing something else. Every time I'd get to the end of the block, I'd make believe I was talking to my brother Allie. I'd say to him, "Allie, don't let me disappear, don't let me disappear, don't let me disappear, please Allie."[9]

Salinger's character gave voice to what many teenagers experience during this time of identity-model formation: "I seem to be taking shape to myself but I don't have a firm grip yet." Most of us are able to survive those years with the fourth circle of modeling well on its way to being complete.

The sixth circle of models includes models of the significant human relationships that make up our ecology of spirit. This cluster refers to the powerful matrix within which and out of which our identity emerges. Here are models of family, kinship, friendship, neighbor, and community, and the way one should operate within these relationships. These are our MODELS OF HUMAN COMMUNITY.

The seventh circle of models contains VALUES MODELS. This circle includes ideals of behavior and criteria for judging the value of the events, persons, things and relationships. It includes models of what is right and wrong, ugly and beautiful, helpful and hurtful. This circle is the residence of one's life-stance or "manifesto." It feeds one's self model by defining the values one chooses to incarnate. It is the system of good and bad that guides our actions.

The eighth circle includes MODELS OF HISTORY and the meaning of the flow of time. They include expectations of how events unfold. They connect one's personal life story with a larger social chronicle. This circle of models includes assumptions about the forces of history, the cycles of history, and a generalized feel for the direction or character of history.

The ninth circle includes MODELS OF THE FUTURE. This circle includes scripts or life plans, dreams for the future, hopes for the world and predictions about what's next. One's models of the future are built out of the stuff of the inner circles and in turn help to form the way we perceive the details that are processed by the inner circles.

Finally, the tenth circle holds MODELS OF THE COSMOS. They include conclusions and assumptions about the nature of creation, God, evolution, the purpose of creation and the place of the human spirit in the whole of creation. This larger circle is the residence of some of our religious models and cosmological beliefs.

The dynamo for these models of the world is the interaction of raw experience with a brain. The brain must put the data together into meaningful patterns and models because it is the models of the world by which and in which we live and move and have our being.

HOW THE CIRCLES OF MODELING
GROW AND CHANGE

The most striking difference between a circle of radiating ripples in a pool and the circles of models is that when a rock splashes into a pool, it is not long before the pool is again flat, but the ripples in the pool of models are slow to dissipate. The mind holds its impressions. They form according to these three principles:

1. The circles of models grow from the central "splash" out. ALL the models we carry around with us are, to varying degrees, the product of sensual data splashing into our pools.[10]

Our self-images, the communities we claim, the values we hold dear, the visions we have for the future and the stance we take toward the world *find their origins in specific sensory events.* That does not mean we can't learn about some abstract concept without going through all the specific experiences that the originator of the concept had. Rather, it means we can understand abstractions now because of the years of experiences that have gone into creating personal models. I can read a book on music theory and learn new things about music because there is enough correspondence between the theory I am reading about and my own experiences with music that allows me to comprehend. The basis of all one's models of the world is personal experiences. When we begin our lives, those things sensed are all we have to define experiences. But as a baby begins to build models of his or her physical world, the *models* begin to be what he or she relates to. And so it is for the rest of one's life.

2. The models of the outer circles tend to control how we perceive new experiences. What we see, hear, smell, taste, and touch is as much a product of what we *expected* as it is a product of what first reached our senses.

The older we get, the harder it is to keep the outer five circles of models from directing our senses to perceive what is expected. The more we have concluded about the world, the faster we recognize things and the more often we leap to wrong conclusions.[11]

3. Breaking the "tyranny" of belief that keeps us from appreciating new ideas or comprehending novel experiences happens from the center of the pool out. That means that our minds are changed by repeated experiences that do not fit old models. The new data may finally overwhelm old ideas.

MODELS OF THE OUTER CIRCLES: MANIFESTO

Consider again the parallel between memory and quilts. Simply stated, our warehouse of memories is like the heritage quilt. The heritage quilt was a sewing together of events, values and beliefs into a cloth integrity. Its unity was in the way the blocks of symbols added up to a "meta-symbol" of a person's life. The quilt was a manifesto of the person it represented. (I am indebted to Dr. Ross Snyder for reclaiming the "manifesto concept.") So it is with the warehouse of memory. Our memories are not isolated episodes and models floating in our heads without integrity. Instead, human memory takes shape because a fresh event hooks a memory to form a new but connected one. Or, if the new event cannot be reconciled with some part of our stock of knowledge and models, our minds will go to great lengths to make a fit (even if means ignoring the facts). There is plenty of evidence to suggest that there is no memory in our minds that does not share in the interconnectedness of the whole. I do not mean that all we think and know has logical connections with everything else. Instead, all we think and know is linked together as one "quilt." The pattern of these elusive but essential threads of integrity are what I want to call one's manifesto. The quilt is but one of the countless media we humans use to manifest our selves in the world.[12]

This manifesto is a slippery thing. It can be talked about but it is difficult to define. It takes shape out of the many models of the world that we create in our lifetime. It reflects one's culture, it includes one's posture toward living and toward other people, it is stamped with our personality and identity, it conforms to core values we hold, and it is distorted by our fears. Our manifesto is our faith, our hope, our theme. It is the sort of thing that epitaphs and obituaries point to. It is what biographers try to capture and what our face and posture reveal. It is made of the outer circles of our models: identity, relationships, values, futures, historical perspective and cosmic vision.

As a religious educator, I am concerned with the processes of cognition, and not just because I need to know the best ways to help a person remember the names of the twelve disciples or the Ten Commandments. I am concerned about cognition because it holds important keys of understanding how to nurture the unfolding of a person's manifesto—a manifesto that can be redemptive both for the person and for the social ecology in which one exists. It behooves us to become familiar with the cognitive processes that are at work as we manufacture our models of the world. In the next chapter we will turn to some strategies for doing education that take processes seriously.

CHAPTER THREE

The Role of the Religious Educator/Factory Consultant

SIX WAYS TO EDUCATE

IF THE BRAIN can be compared to a factory, then how might we think of the job of the religious educator in this metaphor? Think of the educator as a factory consultant. As a consultant is to a factory, so the educator is to the learner/meaning-maker. Like an expert who is invited in to streamline a factory, locate raw materials or assist in product development, the religious educator is one who is invited into the learner's world of meaning to assist in the development of his or her models of the world. The educator represents a stream of meaning and history passed from generation to generation as religious culture. As it was a gift to the educator, so it is presented as gift to the learner—raw material to another pilgrim. The consultant works in any one or combination of six functions meant to bring the factory to full production: as developer, trainer, source of needed information, example, encourager and outfitter.

These six ways of consulting correspond to six educational traditions stemming from the definition of Educator:

Consider the traditions of these roles in the words themselves. The word *educator* is from the latin *educe:* to draw out; from *educare:* to evolve, to rear, to bring up, to develop. To educate is to help a person gather what he or she knows and what he or she needs to know in order to grow up.[1]

Add to that definition the definition of *religion*. The dictionary reveals something of the background of the word. *Religion* is from the Latin *legare* which means to join or bind (as a ligament joins bone and muscle). Literally, it means to bind back or reconnect. One's religion is that which reconnects us with what is elemental and ultimate.[2]

A religious educator, then, is the one who delivers and draws out the memories, urges, information and experiences that serve to reconnect a person with what is at the heart of creation, with ultimacy. At least six strategies

35

for doing this have emerged from human history: by (1) rearing, (2) teaching, (3) informing, (4) equipping, (5) training, and (6) nurturing. These summarize the work or the religious educator/factory consultant.

Consider the roots of these other words humanity has invented to describe the work of the educator.

Nurture is from the Latin word *nurse:* to suckle, feed, release milk in the required trickle. Similarly, *nourish* means to feed and sustain with that which is necessary for growth. Nurture, then, refers to the feeding and sustaining actions that promote the natural process of growth.[3] We are meaning factories that are alive and growing. Living organisms require food and conditions that promote aliveness and growth. Any religious educator who does not promote and participate in the organic, spiritual, emotional growth needs of a person will fail to educate for growth. To believe in the importance of nurture is to believe in each person's God given plan for growth, a plan that is more etched in the chromosomes of the person than is imposed from the outside. It is to respect each person's ability to name his or her own needs and meet them. It is to see the person as whole, that is, to affirm the indivisible nature of a person. Our physical, emotional, relational, intellectual and spiritual needs are all interconnected, requiring education to address all of these elements—often all at the same time. To believe in nurture is to believe that love, affection, grace, and challenge help people grow a workable manifesto and a mature attitude toward God.

Toyohiko Kagawa: Nurturer

Toyohiko Kagawa was born on July 10, 1888, in Japan. Early in his life he was convinced that he was called to be a follower of Jesus. Of all that Jesus was to him, it was his compassion to which the young Toyohiko was drawn. It was no surprise to those who knew him when Toyohiko decided to extend a ministry of presence, education and medicine to the poor in the Shinkawa slums near Kobe. The poor of Shinkawa were the poorest of the poor. Disease and malnutrition was the way of life in these slums. People died by the scores each day. Like Jesus, the young Kagawa was drawn to the needs of the poor and disenfranchised.

As a follower of Jesus, Toyohiko wanted to bring these people to know of the love of God in a way that he knew. He wanted to teach them about compassion, justice and hope. To his astonishment, no religious movement or public institution had any mission to the slums. Facing an overwhelming task, he dug in and prepared to salvage his friends in Shinkawa.

His early efforts made it clear that he did not have the skills or knowledge for the tasks, so he went to the United States where Toyohiko enrolled at Princeton University and earned his degree. He returned not only a more committed disciple, but a skilled social reformer as well. He was ordained in 1917 in Japan.

He and his wife moved to the slums permanently. It did not take him long to discover that food, medicine and clothing would have to be the vessel of good news to his brothers and sisters in the slums. Before a creed was learned or soul converted, minds and bodies had to be made whole. Kagawa's ministry was the work of nutritionist, nurse, doctor and grocer. The only clear way he could offer hope was to feed, heal and clothe.

In his years of caring, writing, being a political force and working for justice with those people of the slums, he became world famous for his ministry: the simple and powerful presence of incarnate love that shouts the gospel by nursing, nurturing, writing, going to jail and speaking out for the castoffs of the slums. Kagawa risked his life and health daily drinking contaminated water, eating rancid food and living closely with nearly every contagious disease known to humanity. His work in the slums cost him his sight and finally his life. He died in 1960. To those he nurtured, regardless of their religion, he gave his full measure of humanity, helping people to reconnect with what is at the heart of creation and of every creative, nurturing act.

Once he wrote, "Love awakens all it touches. Love whispers in the ear and arouses the heart. . . . The sanctuary of God is love. I know that I can worship God only in love."[4]

* * *

To *train* is from Middle English and means to draw on, to drag, or trail.[5] It refers to the activities a trainer employs to help a trainee turn what he or she understands into a skill. The trainer draws or drags the pieces of a skill out into manageable, practical steps and usable knowledge. Consider the work of a diving coach. He or she is able to break a dive into its many steps or pieces. As the diver learns these dive operations, they become automatic. Finally, the coach helps the diver "train" these steps into one complex motion. If the trainer has done well and the diver possesses the natural ability and strength, the dive seems an almost effortless, seamless action—an expression of grace and beauty.

In religious education there are many skills that students can be trained to turn into actions of their own. These can be intellectual skills (scripture study, writing, keeping a journal), interpersonal skills (effective listening, speaking, playing fair), spiritual skills (praying, meditating, worshiping), artistic skills (painting, creative writing, singing, dancing) or even physical skills (the skill of an acolyte or caring for babies). Skills other than academic ones are often overlooked in curriculum that emphasizes information learning. More than once I have listened to a teacher report how a quiet or difficult child has found a new level of self-esteem and competence simply by discovering a religious skill he or she can master.

Martha Snyder: Player-Coach of Young Children

Martha and Ross Snyder were pioneers in religious education. During their long tenure at Chicago Theological Seminary, they were redefining the work of the Christian educator, skillfully wedding the arts, communications theory, cultural anthropology and sociology into workable, effective models for doing youth and children's ministry.

Martha aimed her educational gifts toward ministry with young children and the training of adult workers in early childhood education. Under her guidance, the seminary housed one of the most creative and effective schools for young children in the nation. It was (and still is) a lab for teachers and a support for parents and provided a rich spiritual ecology for children. Although it was a teaching school for university students pursuing a vocation in early childhood education, Martha never stopped teaching the children. Martha kept verbatim accounts of her conversations and encounters with the children of the nursery school and included many of them in a book that she, her son and her husband wrote together called *The Young Child as Person*.

Reading her experiences and hearing her talk about the respect with which she held children and the value she placed on them is inspiring. But even more awesome was the skill with which Martha trained university students to be competent and loving teachers. Her method had at the heart of its design the practice reflection rhythm of the field approach to learning. Students were expected to learn a full repertoire of skills needed to work with children—from listening to refereeing, from storytelling to celebrating, from psychological assessment to referral, from parent conferencing to family intervention.

Martha was a player-coach sort of trainer who first demonstrated these skills to the students, observed and gave feedback to them as they practiced, led seminars that used the school experiences as the heart of their reflection, and then encouraged the sort of research that put their skills into the pedagogical and theological context that gave these skills deeper purpose and meaning.

Martha trained them as intensely as if she were training long-distance runners. The results were always valuable. Her students graduated as master teachers and as more mature human beings. Whether with children or university students, she was always a loving and respectful presence who lured the best from others. Martha Snyder, one of God's trainers.[6]

* * *

To *rear* is from an Anglo Saxon word meaning to put upright by pushing from behind, to elevate, to erect, to grow.[7] By implication, to rear is to encourage. All growth contains elements of risk, and so part of what it means to be a religious educator is to encourage a student to face the difficulties of growth encountered along his or her spirit journey. This "rear action" empowers a person to take on new experiences and their meaning. In the process, the student is reared closer to God and neighbor. Listening, encouraging, counseling, praising, and challenging are all part of the repertoire of the religious educator and fit this function of "rearing."

Paul Irwin: The Power to Encourage

Dr. Paul Irwin is professor emeritus of Christian Education at the School of Theology at Claremont, California. Although an effective and inspiring lecturer, Paul knew only too well the limitations of speech. What makes him a delight as a teacher and a friend is his ability to encourage students to discover. I like to think of Paul as a doorman. He opens the door for his students to concepts and strategies that turn students into teachers. For me and my classmates, Paul opened the door to Erik Erikson and the developmental approach to learning, encouraging us to enter. He opened the door to Joseph Campbell and the power of myth, encouraging us to come in. He swung the doors wide to the human potential movement, multicultural Christian education, and to group dynamics, encouraging us to step inside. If the doorway couldn't be opened in class, he would take his classes to door-openings all over Southern California: Pacific Oaks School, parochial schools, East Los Angeles public schools, churches, Montessori schools, and even Patton State Hospital for the mentally disabled. Paul knew that any one of us could discover what makes for effective education, that all we needed was opportunity and encouragement. Of all the teachers I have had, he is the one who helped me find the courage to be a teacher. Paul believed in me and in all his students. That's what doormen do—they open a way for us and trust us to step through.

* * *

To *inform* is from the Latin *in* + *forma*, meaning "to shape." As a noun *in-form* means the character of a thing that gives it shape.[8] ("Your character," by the way, according to evil Dr. Lazardo in the film *Buckaroo Banzai*, "is what you are in the dark.") As a verb it means to build up from the inside, in order for a thing or person to appear or take shape. What is information, then, but the stuff we inform each other with. Consider all the information that goes into us; then wonder at the shape we take. Religious traditions are deep vessels of information and the educator is a custodian and transmitter of that information. From the stories of scripture to the traditions of the history of one's religion, from values to courtesies, from language to symbols—this is the stuff of one's religious culture. The skillful informing educator is the one who can deliver the culture, instruct a student on its value and use, and then help him or her to contribute to and transform it to be relevant to the present. It is important to never lose track of the purpose of in-formation: to form a person from the inside. The character-building happens when the student claims the culture as his or her own model of how life and living works.

Rabbi Hillel, the Elder: In-forming Character

The time of Roman occupation and dominance of Judah in the first centuries B.C.E. and C.E. was a time that could have seen the demise of the Jewish culture. Were it not for the faithfulness of key rabbis and pharisees of that time, the great traditions and the institutions of learning in Judah would have crumbled. Just before the ministry of the rabbi Jeshua ben Joseph, in the vicinity of the Sea of Galilee, other rabbis risked much to reclaim the traditions of the Torah and interpret the Law. A Talmudic sage and leading scholar in the development of the oral tradition taught during that difficult time. He was Rabbi Hillel the Elder (60 B.C.E.–20 C.E.). The founder of the academy that bore his name, Hillel devoted his life to the interpretation to the Law and to reclaiming the culture and religion of the Torah. He knew that a person's character grows from the inside out and that the Law and Prophets were for the formation of the character of righteous and faithful people.

He was famous both as a kind and saintly presence and as a scholar and gifted teacher. The stories of his life as a rabbi show us a teacher well acquainted with the value of spirited dialogue between student and teacher, and also shows us the power of love, affection and patience in the building of character. Some of the stories put him in conflict with another more strict and unbending rabbi, Shammai. Once, when Shammai rebuffed a student asking about the essence of the Torah, Hillel took the student and his question with seriousness. His answer to the young man is now a part of Talmudic Wisdom: "What is the essence of the Torah, you ask? Whatever is hateful to you do not do to your fellow. This is the whole Torah; all else is commentary. Go and learn that."

To this day Hillel is a model of the teacher who passionately delivered the traditions of the past in a way that allows them to inform us for today.[9]

* * *

To *equip* is from the French word *esquiper*, which means to embark, to make ready to put out to sea, to outfit (rather than to in-form), to dress.[10] The consultant may be required to bring new resources to a factory or recommend new equipment to get the job done. Just so, the religious educator needs to be ready to outfit the student with tools and resources for the journey of spirit, the pilgrimage of faith. It may be a book, a map, a picture, a degree, a supporting group, a motto, a letter of recommendation, or a benediction. Whatever the resource turns out to be, its purpose is to serve the student in the quest for maturity.

Madeleine L'Engle: Outfitting Spiritual Pilgrims

You probably know her as a story writer. Madeleine L'Engle's *Wrinkle In Time* is one of the most popular children's novels of the decade. Her books for adults, such as *Everyday Prayers, The Genesis Trilogy* and *The Love Letters,* speak to the pilgrim in us.

Madeleine was born in 1918 in New York City. Books and stories were part of her life from the beginning. So was her church. Both have been and are resources for her spiritual pilgrimage. All her books assume that we are adventurers, and that faith and spirituality have more to do with how we travel, adventure and discover than they do with right belief or correct disciplines. Her readers find in her stories ideas, lives and resources they can stuff into their backpacks as tools and resources for their own spirit journeys.

Besides being a writer, Madeleine is a resident lay theologian at her church in New York. Her vocation there has to do with helping others discover the equipment they need for their journey of growth and maturity. Such is the theme in her stories, lectures and small-group gatherings: listen for the call to go forward, respond to it and don't forget to take the skills, books, memories, stories and disciplines that will see you through. Why? Because change is constant; in change we meet whatever is at the heart of things, and in change we will meet ourselves. "To be human," she wrote, "is to be able to change, knowing full well that some change is good and some is bad; some change is regressive and some progressive, and we cannot often discern which is which. But if we lose the ability to change, we stultify, we turn to stone, we die." [11]

* * *

To *teach* is from the Anglo Saxon root *tot* or *taecon*, meaning sign or symbol. To teach is to show or demonstrate using pointers, analogies, signs and symbols.[12] All of education is something of an art form, but this way of teaching requires an especially creative mind and a playful joy in finding interesting and powerful ways to point to the sacred in the mundane. In the process, the teacher models a skill we all need: using metaphors and analogies to wring sense out of experience. But it means more: the powerful "teacher" becomes the "token," the model for religious fidelity and aliveness and a call forward to deeper and broader living.

Mohandas Gandhi: A Life that Instructs

Mohandas K. Gandhi, like Toyohiko Kagawa and Martin Luther King, Jr., came to his self-understanding as an educator because he cared so deeply for the powerless and disenfranchised of his time and country. He was a product of that part of India where religious traditions washed over a person's life like the waves of the Indian Ocean on the shores of that subcontinent. Religious influences came from every hemisphere, each with its own direction, power and shape, and each moving the spiritual sands of India's cultures. Gandhi was a man who embraced human religion with a conviction that each was a wave made of the same water.

Gandhi was a lawyer, a member of an occupied nation, a Hindu, a British subject and, finally, a brother to us all. The story of his pilgrimage from his homeland to England, to South Africa, and home again is a long and full one. What is striking about his life is that his themes of self-development, freedom, religious tolerance, respect for all humans, and non-violent political action were convincing. They convinced not because of their uniqueness, but because he modeled those virtues so completely. His life taught, his actions instructed, his being was teacher.[13]

(In Figure 3.1 these six strategies are arranged on a wheel representing the work of the religious educator. There are few who could claim expertise in all six, so do not conclude that I think an educator must be proficient or even interested in all. I do think, however, that in our churches and temples, teams of teachers,

counselors, nurturers, and so on, ought to pool their talents and interests for the sake of the education, formation and maturation of faithful people.)

PILGRIM'S PROGRESS
IN THE FAITH COMMUNITY

Anthropologist Joseph Campbell compared a person's life to that of a mythological pilgrim or hero. He likened our lives to an *inner* hero journey. His *Hero With a Thousand Faces* documents the universal character of this "hero Journey" motif in human psyche and culture.[14] It is the story of one who hears a call to new and deeper life for the sake of each pilgrim's growth as well as for the sake of his people. Those with the courage to respond to the growth opportunity embark on a pilgrimage, or "hero journey." The pilgrim myth is a metaphor for us. Any growth is like this model of the pilgrim (see Chapter 11 for a fuller discussion of the "Pilgrim Motif").

No one teacher or guide will be able to serve a pilgrim through every stage of his or her pilgrimage. The nurturer sometimes must give way to the

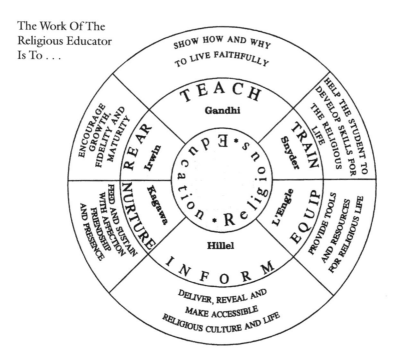

The Work Of The Religious Educator Is To . . .

Figure 3.1 The Work of the Religious Educator

challenger; the in-former must sometimes step aside for the equiper. The kind of educator/consultant a person needs most depends on what part of the pilgrimage he or she is on. This is one of the reasons spiritual pilgrims need a spiritual base camp such as their community of faith. Within its culture there are many teachers, educators and meaning-consultants to share the task of calling student pilgrims toward maturity and communion with the Heart of things.

These six educational strategies are best implemented by the educator/ consultant who profoundly respects and appreciates the unique world of meaning created by the learner. No matter how involved the educator/consultant becomes in the learner's process of meaning-making, the models of the world always belong to the learner. To use the trust a student places in an educator to claim, control or corrupt that world of meaning is the pinnacle of cynicism and the deadliest of sins. To be an educator is to be, prior to all else, one who has a passion to let the student be. Martha Snyder uses the word *presence* to point to the respect all educators should seek to establish with a student. She described this relationship in the book she wrote with her son and husband about young children:

> I am here, right in this situation, not paying attention to anyone else or anything else but you. I am for you, with you, and on the side of your growth. To me you are not a problem to solve or a discipline case. You are not clay to be shaped. You are a momentum, a power, a spirit that is utterly fascinating. I accept you as a fellow human whom I believe in, no matter how much we may disagree. No matter how hard we struggle, we will always get back together. Every so often I am lost in wonder, amazement, and delight when we meet.[15]

CHAPTER FOUR

Religious Education
as Model Building

I HAVE ARGUED that meaning-making is the first priority of the cortex. It works like a factory that combines several cognitive systems and programs to make sense of the world each person encounters. In that meaning-making enterprise, humans have looked to each other for help in making sense of the world. We educate each other. I have described six ways we have traditionally helped each other make sense of life in the context of religion and the human pilgrimage. Now I want to get more specific about strategies and curricula that cognitive science shows to be most effective.

TRUST THE STUDENT

Morton Hunt, in his descriptive volume about the way people model the world, calls the brain's product "The Universe Within." He argues that since the cortical tissue holds working models of the world and of how to act in it, the basic study of cognition ought to be a study of the programs, protocols, and processes that make model-building possible. Hunt cites study after study supporting this key insight: each brain is a natural expert at discovering patterns, categories, concepts and meaning. We impede that expertise by imposing the conclusions of others without offering the raw experiences the conclusions rest on. People do better at discovering meaning when they don't have to deal with ready-made conclusions handed over by an instructor.[1] This is what I call the **First Principle of Cognitive Ethic** (see Table 4.1).

Think of a child just learning to talk and name things. Imagine the child being exposed to a wide variety of containers with flat bottoms, open at one end and with handles. Now imagine the child using them with other people who know what they are for and what they are called. Soon that child will be able to identify each of the individual containers by its class name and use

Table 4.1
The First Principle of Cognitive Ethic:
The Student is the Expert at Making Meaning.
The Educator Assists the Student by:

Providing Rich Experiences	Encouraging Border-Crossing	Encouraging Complete Meaning-Making
Plan to let students hear encounters between people representing opposing points of view Using debates, arguments, reenactments.	Cross cultural borders through travel, foreign guests, cultural exhibits, study tours.	Connect experiences with all the circles of meaning by asking relevant questions related to the levels of meaning;
Plan to let students encounter people and ideas of the past through movies, plays, biographies, books.	Cross time borders by visiting museums, digs, viewing videos, taking historical tours. Cross economic borders through plunge experiences, work teams, exchanges, dialogue groups.	encouraging students to express the meanings of experiences through the arts; encouraging students to write their affirmations of faith or manifestoes;
Plan to let students encounter artistic expressions about an idea or experience by encountering the arts, doing art, showing art.	Cross biological borders through exchanges, visits, dialogue with people who are physically different (gender, race, size, ability).	encouraging students to preach or teach about the meanings they affirm; providing ways for the student to encounter the lives of people who have uncovered meaning in ordinary moments, who see the everyday with fresh eyes;
Plan to encourage students to step back from an issue, to be detectives, scientists and critics by keeping a journal, taking notes, being observers, making documentaries, writing a report.	Cross political borders by attending a rally, reading another view. Cross religious borders by attending other worships, reading another religion's scripture.	encouraging fantasy and imagination.

each correctly. Let's say that one of the classes of containers is "cup." Using it, seeing it in use, and hearing it being called "cup" is enough for a child (or anyone) to build in his or her mind a stereotype of "cupness." Without ever having heard the definition of "cup," the child will be able to describe cupness and be able to differentiate a cup from a pitcher or glass. The accuracy of the child's descriptions and choices is directly proportional to the experience of using cups, glasses and pitchers, not to his or her ability to recite a definition. In fact, one of the impediments to establishing a useful model of "cupness" is the imposition, on the part of teachers, of the definition before the experience. Experience and involvement with the category is the best teacher. These experiences are stored in ways that automatically organize them into classes and categories.[2]

The same principle applies to the learning of more abstract or complex classes of experience. Religious, philosophical and ethical classes and categories get classified too. Students will naturally develop religious and theological concepts based upon the experiences they have had. This means that the key to the teaching of theological and ethical concepts is the quality and quantity of experiences with those concepts and meanings. If I want students to define the nature of human beings, they must experience the richness of humanity. I, as teacher, have as my first task that of arranging the "circle of experiences" (the definition of *curriculum*) that would constitute a well-rounded and honest glimpse of human behavior. They will take the curriculum and add to what they already know about people.

The thrust of the **First Principle** is that the teacher must avoid the temptation to deliver the goods ready-made. To do so will interfere with natural process by which an idea, meaning or concept takes shape in the memory network of the student. The student will do better without having to fit his or her experiences to a teacher's conclusions.

This does not mean that I, as a teacher, should refrain from revealing my own model of the world. Just the opposite is true. Besides being a deliverer of information, the teacher himself or herself is part of what is delivered. The educator needs to be careful not to shove those models into a student's world of meaning. Rather, the teacher needs to share those models as part of the alternatives. Trust the truth to reveal itself to the brains of the students hungry for meaning.

If I may mix metaphors again, as one gives birth to a new model of part of the world, a good midwife is called for. This is a person who will help the birth happen naturally, but with guiding hands and clear instructions.

The teacher-consultant-midwife is the one who helps the new model get born, applying a five-part teaching ethic:

1. Thou shalt ACTIVELY LISTEN. Thanks to Carl Rogers[3] and Gordon Thomas,[4] the power of listening actively and carefully has been dramatically demonstrated. Active listening is a way of paying attention by reflecting back to the one speaking the emotional and intellectual content of what was said. Such mirroring of what a person communicates is a powerful feedback medium that allows a person to think twice about the meaning shared. When someone is in the process of clarifying a thought, it is the sort of listening that speeds up the process and aids thinking. Active listening is one of the most powerful tools a teacher can use.

2. Thou shalt COMPARE AND CONTRAST. Almost as powerful in the clarification of ideas is the chance to see one's thought or model alongside a similar one and to discover how the two "fit." A teacher who can place an alternate idea alongside another idea offers the student a chance to discover insights that wouldn't happen without the juxtaposition.

3. Thou shalt encourage QUESTIONING. A variation of comparing is simply the art of raising questions. A question that asks the student to apply his or her idea to some concrete situation or to project it into the future can help identify its strength and weakness. These are "what if" and "what about when" questions.

4. Thou shalt be an EXAMPLE OF A PERSON TRYING NEW WAYS OF EXPRESSION. We all have our favorite ways of letting others know what we mean. For me it is with photographs. However, if that was the only way I communicated, I would not get much "said." I am thankful to teachers in my past who have led me to say what I think in more than one way. In most cases, these teachers modeled to me the willingness to find more than one or two "voices." When we are able to say, draw and even sing an idea, the idea's richness or weakness becomes more apparent. The more we can lure students to express their ideas in a variety of media, the better the chance that their ideas will get tested for fidelity.

5. Thou shalt be an EYEWITNESS. Each of us has seen things, experienced life and felt the movement of the divine in unique ways. These are the things that we teachers are expert in. No good teacher will deprive students of this witness. We ought not believe that ours is the only or best of models of reality, but at the same time it is the one *we know* best. Witness to the way the universe has taken shape in yourself.

The **First Principle** not only demands a certain teaching ethic, it implies at least these strategies for educators:

1. Humans learn best from a curriculum of rich personal experience rather than from a curriculum of someone else's conclusions. The one most potent curriculum strategy a teacher can employ for the benefit of learners is to let students experience everything possible related to a subject.[5]

2. Another powerful teaching/learning strategy is border-crossing. The one who seeks out other perspectives, cultural slants and disciplines is the one whose world models are the more durable and trustworthy.

3. Finally, educational strategy ought to encourage persons to think about the implications experiences have for both the "physical" and "meta physical" levels of meaning. Models are formed as we weave our experiences in with meanings at all nine levels of models. Biology, for example, has value in itself but its ripples cannot help but spread into our models of self, values, relationships, futures, and the cosmos. Pedagogical strategy ought to include plans to help a student reflect on the meaning experiences and subjects have for all our models of the world.

Consider each of these strategies as they might illuminate the task of Religious Education.

PLANNING RICH CURRICULA

The ideal way to think and decide would be to present all the facts before a person makes up his or her mind about how the world works. Obviously it can't be done. There is no way that human beings can have all the facts about the world, and no way that we can be kept from leaping to conclusions. However, many facts, stories and experiences are better than a few, so let us plan curricula to be as rich as we can imagine and manage. The temptation is to plan experiences for our students that are just reruns of our own. Such is neither appropriate nor effective. Let me offer these guidelines that might lead to a richer curriculum of experience:

1. Plan experiences that allow students to see different perspectives and points of view. Let's take the issue of human nature considered by a class of adults or older youth students. Part of a lesson plan could include encounters with the thinkers who represent the many philosophies of human nature in face-to-face dialogue. If there is a college or university near by, use their resources and people.

In a class of preadolescents studying the biblical account of creation, a scientist describing evolution, for example, can encourage students to take a fresh look at the meaning of God as creator. In a group of preschoolers learning about prayer, introducing a variety of ways to pray can help the children claim prayer as their own discipline.

The strategies need to be appropriate to age and culture, but encouraging a fresh perspective is an instructive and liberating strategy.

2. Plan encounters with events, ideas and people of the past. Much of what can be said about any topic has been said, so plan encounters with

events and thinkers who have gone before. Showing documentaries on video, reenacting events, role-playing lives of historical figures, recreating environments of times long past—all of these enrich students' experience and contribute to model building. Every age group can benefit from educational time travel.

3. Plan to present a variety of artistic expressions of a concept, event, feeling or fact. All of what has been expressed about life has been expressed in some form of art. Therefore, we must not neglect the arts (sculpture, painting, music, literature, film, and the like). Every age group can access some level of meaning and feeling of great painting, sculpture, and music. So why not incorporate Van Gogh's "Starry Night" in a lesson about the sky with young children? Why not plan a trip to a museum to see a replica of Michelangelo's "David" while learning about the creation of the nation of Israel with young teens?

4. Plan ways to help the student to step back from what is going on. This is the skill of being an observer. Asking students to comment on the learning process or asking questions of them about the motivations of people invites them to take a detached view for a moment. Even young children can do this. Asking questions of a preschooler about what another child or even a cultural hero feels or wants can encourage this "stepping back."

5. Plan for the student to collect and share his or her own experiences related to the concept. It is a mistake to teach a student to value *other* insights and experience over his or her own. Both are valuable and both are fragmented without the other. Thus, it is important to the richness of a curriculum to include methods for personal reflection and meditation. Journal keeping, poetry writing, drawing, dramatic play, and sculpting all facilitate reflection and sharing.

CROSSING BORDERS

When I think of the ancient Hebrews, it makes sense to me that theirs was a culture that developed ethical monotheism. Their religious journey brought them a step or two closer to an understanding of how the universe works and how social systems survive. They were the "border-crossers" (which is a translation of the root of the word *Hebrew*). As such, they contacted and were able to survive in a number of cultures. As these nomads moved through the ethical, religious, and cultural contradictions of the social systems of the Middle East, they benefited. The benefit was a result of the opportunity to compare cultures, to accumulate information, to learn an openness to other traditions, and to test their models of the world on a larger scale than was possible for societies sunk into river beds. The Hebrews were able to get their experiential "arms" around more of the world and to form a world model with a greater degree of fidelity.

I propose that education ought to take students across at least four kinds of borders in search of a more complete model of the world as follows:

1. Help students **cross cultural borders** to answer, "How do other groups of human beings understand this part of life?" Taking part in study tours, hosting foreign guests, hearing reports from travelers, watching films, using artifacts and visiting exhibits from other cultures—all are methods for crossing cultural borders. What borders are crossed and what kind of crossing will need to fit the age and experience of the students.

2. Help students **cross time borders** to answer, "How did people understand this part of life in the past?" Archeological digs, videos, historical pageants, historical tours, museum trips, art and literature study are all methods for crossing time borders. Again, how students are introduced to the past needs to be appropriate for their age and experience.

3. Help students **cross economic borders** to answer, "How does economic status effect one's understanding and experience of life?" Plunge experiences, work teams, exchanges, role-playing or helping at a soup kitchen are some ways of crossing economic borders. Being poor or rich are conditions on which even the youngest students can have a grasp. Likewise, a person of any age can think of the rich or poor as "them" or "us." Crossing borders can enlarge our circle of "us."

4. Help students **cross biological borders** to answer, "How do (men, women, blacks, whites, browns, young, old, handicapped, and so forth) people I can never be like understand this part of life?" Sharing, friendships, dialogue, play groups are methods for crossing these biological borders. The spirit of this approach is captured in this poem by an unknown brother or sister:

THE SHAPE OF GOD

May you who would know
The true shape of God
Be bent by the wind
And scorched by the sun.
May you taste the salt rock
And chew the sweet rain.
And may you do one more thing:
May you at last look steadfast
Into the eyes of your neighbor.

WEAVING A TIGHTER BASKET

My grandma and grandpa Stout and their twelve children were farmers in North Carolina. My brother and I spent part of our summers with them. I remember some of the many skills my grandma had to master in order to keep the farm operating well. One was weaving various kinds of baskets. In my memory, I have recollections of her weaving on the porch in the evening and telling my brother and me each step in the process while he and I snapped beans. I don't really recall many of the details, but I do remember trying my hand at weaving the strands up through the longitudinal circles of the straw foundation. She would insist that we weave the straw over and under all of the various basket rings that gave the basket its shape. If we didn't, she demonstrated, the basket would lack continuity and strength at the place where a ring was missed. Each pass of the warping straw needed to connect with all the rings or the basket would have a hole, or worse.

This is true of our experiences in relation to our circles of meaning. Try to imagine that the ten circles of models are like the rings that make a basket. They come into being after months of living and become the foundation of one's "basket of meaning." New experiences serve to connect the basket rings and weave them together. New data needs to connect with as many circles of meaning as it will reach so that our warp and woof of meaning might have greater integrity. In fact, when one intentionally weaves new experience around all ten kinds of models, each new experience becomes richer, deeper, and more beautiful.

For example, the fact that Barney Clark could survive as long as he did with a metal and plastic pump in the place of his heart is a challenge to my model of how bodies stay alive (a model of the physical world). But the more challenging aspect of the fact comes as it bends around my set of metaphysical models:

* identity models: (Could *I* still live with myself if *I* had an artificial heart?)
* values models (Is it right to put mechanical organs in a person? Who shall get them?)
* relational models (How do I relate to a person who has an artificial organ?)
* historical models (But this does not fit into my view of history.)
* future models (Where will it end? Will we soon see brains living in machines?)
* cosmic models (What about immortality, God's natural laws, and so forth?)

Too often we try to insulate these outer models from fresh information so as to avoid the sometimes painful implications of the truth: namely that our models must change.

The years since Barney Clark's implant in 1982 have brought more and more medical advances that have to find a place in my "universe within," and then that first artificial heart will no longer seem alien. There will continue to be a lifelong sequence of new things that will have to be woven into my meaning-basket.

When we plan for learning experiences, then, we must look for ways to help students *extend* experiences and data all the way out to the last circles of meaning, *touching* those circles of meaning, *connecting* them to the others and *enriching* them with the new strand of the fabric of life. I want to suggest these ways to do it:

1. *Asking Leading Questions.* Entice the student into a consideration of the larger circles of meaning by asking questions that would focus attention on the issues of those circles. If the learners are older elementary children through adults, help them to become familiar with the circles of modeling and encourage them to discover the questions that each circle would "pose" concerning what is being studied. For younger children you will need to pose the questions yourself or at least be more active in pulling them from the children. Whatever the age, each circle of meaning exists in the minds of the learners and you can facilitate the weaving of their experiences out to the edge by asking questions.

What Questions Are Relevant to Each Circle of Models?

Circle one: Questions about the physical properties of the thing (or event, or person):
What is the shape of this object?

Circle two: Questions about what other objects the thing is like :
What do you call something like this?

Circle three: Questions about the particular thing and its name:
What would you call *this* thing?

Circle four: Questions about where the thing is located and about how it fits with other things over time:
What/where is this place where this thing is?

Circle five: Questions about the way the thing leads me to feel and think about it and about the way it stirs up my self:
Now that I know this thing exists, will I be different?

Circle six: Questions about the value of the thing and of how it will test my values:

Is this good?

Circle seven: Questions about how this thing affects relationships and community life:

What does it mean for those I relate to?

Does it imply something about the way I interact with others?

Does it mean something about those who are my kin?

Circle eight: Questions about how this thing has come to exist:

How could this have come to be?

Circle nine: Questions about how the thing will affect what's next and our understanding of what's next:

What will this thing do to us?

Circle ten: Questions about what the thing shows about what is at the heart of things:

Does this thing's existence tell us that the world is good or bad?

Does it mean there is a creator or creative source?

The reason Galileo's observations about the moons of Jupiter were so earth-shaking was that they called into question all ten circles of meaning. Not only did the observations cast doubt on the model of the solar system (physical circles of meaning), but the circling moons of Jupiter forced questions about time, identity, values, God and our place in creation (the metaphysical circles of meaning). Those who were the custodians of meaning forced him to deny the facts and publicly repudiate what he knew to be the truth. In fact he, and people such as Darwin, Bede, Curie and Pasteur, reshaped religion more than many theologians. They insisted on asking questions about how the physical world held clues to the metaphysical.

2. *Providing examples of persons who pushed everyday experiences and data to deeper or wider circles of meaning.* We need to have easy access to a wide range of biographies of persons with the ability to discern the metaphysical in the ordinary. I don't mean just the great philosophers and scientists; rather I have in mind all kinds of people who saw something in the ordinary that transcended the moment and the senses. The cast for such a repertoire might include Madame Curie, Einstein, Hildegarde of Bingen, Bach, Lao-tzu, and da Vinci. It would also include the elderly woman who lives next door or the young basketball player at the local high school. Whenever we happen upon a person who has a special way of seeing the implica-

tions of the ordinary, we might make a mental note of this person as a resource and model to students. Then, when you can, invite the person into the class. If this isn't possible, visit them or tell their story.

3. *Encouraging fantasy.* Nurture and coax the Don Quixote in students. There is a direct relation between the ability to imagine and the ability to work meaning out of the ordinary. Chapter seven will expand on this idea.

* * *

"I can't believe that!" said Alice. "Can't you?" the Queen said in a pitying tone. "Try again: draw a long breath and shut your eyes." Alice laughed. "There's no use trying," she said: "One can't believe impossible things." "I daresay you haven't had much practice," said the Queen. "When I was your age I always did it for half-an-hour a day. Why, sometimes I believed as many as six impossible things before breakfast."[6]

* * *

Find vivid examples of experiences, facts or discoveries that became pivotal points in the intellectual history of the human drama. Then when you have them, tell them as stories. I have in mind stories about how the discovery of a round world changed our models of the cosmos, or of the way the discovery of microbes changed our scale of the world and of the nature of disease. I also have in mind the "little" discoveries that every person has to make about the size and shape of their world, and how these discoveries explode old models of what is at the heart of things.

SUMMARY

What I have tried to argue is that modeling is the primary work of the cortex. Without its unending work of sorting and combining experience into meaning, the flood of data about the world would simply wash over us. The wonder is that we *do* have this crown of gray matter that recreates the world in its synapses and neural pathways. Modeling does not reduce the flood since the flood is outside our control. Rather, because the cortex allows us to grasp something of the world's nature, it makes it possible for us to ride out the flood. How well we "ride" depends on the seaworthiness of our ship of meaning. All of us can benefit from the help of a pilot who may know more about the waters than do we, who can assist us as we make our own maps of living and being. Teaching and curriculum based on the ethic and strategies of the **First Principle Of Cognitive Ethic** can make the ride more fulfilling for any student.

Next we will consider one of the more detailed but essential mechanisms of the meaning-making process. I refer to the way that meaningful patterns are first separated from the "chaos" of the flood of experience: perception.

CHAPTER FIVE

Perception: Doors
to the Factory

STAR GAZING

STANDING OUTSIDE on clear nights when I was a fifth-grader, I searched the sky with my sky atlas and flashlight in hand, straining to identify the constellations. I wanted to see those same fantastic beings that were drawn on my star map. Trying to locate the constellations that the latest edition of *Sky and Telescope* promised that I could see was sometimes a task larger than the mind of an eleven-year-old could accomplish. I remember thinking, as I strained to see the great Pegasus, that if the ornately-drawn outlines of mythological figures had to be missing from the real sky, whoever was in charge should have at least left in the dotted lines.

Yet there were a few of the "star pictures" that I could locate without much effort: Ursa Major, Sagittarius, Scorpio, and Orion. Their patterns were unmistakable. I remember thinking that even though some of the stars that I had grouped together were missing or organized differently on the official map, my expectations roughly matched the map. Regardless of whether the groupings were those of the map or my own, every star seemed to belong to a group.

It was as if the spring sky was a great domed puzzle that would give up its mysteries when the stargazer was finally able to shake his or her head and see the cosmic pattern that had always been there. The key to solving the sky puzzle had to do with one's ability to see patterns in the star positions, their proximity to each other, the symmetry of their positions, the similarity of brightness or color, plus imagined lines and enclosed areas. In truth, that is exactly what happened: the combined eyes of thousands of years of observers have given to us patterns and figures in the sky based on the groupings and lines that the stars seem to suggest. Even vastly different cultures having very little if any contact with each other have grouped stars in similar ways. What are the cognitive mechanisms common to all human thinking that lead us to organize the sky as we have? Are there similar mechanisms and programs related to the identification of sound patterns? Smells? Touch? Taste? And if there are such protocols and programs resident in every brain, what might that imply about the way we assist persons to build and use models of the world? Might such programs imply a pedagogical outline? Can such an outline instruct us in the tasks of religious education? This will be the focus for this chapter.

Consider this: in the Los Angeles summer sky looking south, three great groupings of stars present themselves. The groupings have come to be called Hercules, Ophiuchus, and Scorpios. Hercules is almost overhead from California at about 10 P.M. and is recognizable as a rectangle of bright stars with several others radiating from it. In the traditional "Ptolemaic" map of the stars, this cluster is named for the Greek god-man Hercules (Figure 5.1). Depending on the artist, the maps present a range of postures of a man holding a weapon. Not unexpectedly, other cultures have drawn different figures around the cluster of stars. To Julius Schiller (in 1627) these same stars represented the three Magi who visited the Baby Jesus,[1] and to some ancient Greek mapmakers, the cluster was simply named for a geometric figure. What is interesting is that cultures from many different parts of the world group the stars in almost the same sets. The "Big Dipper" may resemble a ladle to some or the body of a bear to others, but to all of us the seven stars seem to be related. The same is true of the Constellation "Leo." In the standard European star map, it represents a lion. In the ancient Egyptian culture it represented the Sphinx. In early European maps, it was a sickle.[2] The star

Hercules

Figure 5.1

maps of the world's cultures, then, reveal basic perceptual mechanisms or ways that human beings group visual information: by proximity, by similarity, and by symmetry.

HOW TO SEE THE GODS AND HEAR FEELINGS

There are at least five "loading docks" into the brain factory's receiving department: the sense of vision (the perception of light, dark, shades of gray and color), the sense of hearing, the sense of taste (roughly four qualities of taste), the sense of smell (which combines with taste to cause the sensation of flavor), and the sense of touch (hot, cold, pain, pressure, texture, and so forth). They can be divided into three groups depending on their range: long range or "tele-sensors" (sight, and hearing), medium range (smell), and close range or contact sensors (the touch/pain group, and taste). All are methods of receiving information and delivering that information to the brain so that it can be understood. Each species of animal relies on different combinations of senses. Consequently, we will find one animal's sense of smell highly developed (as in the case of the bloodhound), while another has a highly developed sense of sight (as in the case of a barn owl). Still others develop variations that seem to be altogether different senses (as in the case of a snake's ability to sense changes in infrared radiation caused by the presence of warm-blooded animals).

Whether there are five or fifteen, our senses keep us in touch with the environment within which we must find the sources of life. For adult human beings, the long-range senses have become our busiest loading docks. The shapes, colors, contours, features and designs that we see and the tones, sequences, noises and timbre that we hear carry the heaviest cargo of meaning. The amount of cortex area and the number of neurons given over to the receiving and processing of visual information are greater than for any other sensory organ.[3] A distant second is the cortex area given to the processing of sound. Thus, for you and me, the keys to perception can be found in the examination of the ways we see and hear. If we consider the ways pictures of gods are "seen" in the night sky and the way feelings are stirred by musical sound, I suggest that we will be able to isolate the principles that operate in the moment of perception. I would further suggest that these same perception principles are at work at every circle of meaning described in the previous chapter. That is to say that the organizing principles that make it possible to detect features at the physical level are at work in the detection of meaning at the meta-physical level. The programs that organize stars into patterns and

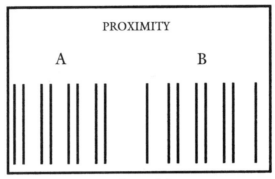

Figure 5.2

sounds into music and words are the same programs that allow us to sense our identities, relationships, history, time, value, and the integrity of the cosmos.

Then what are they? What are the principles of perception that lead us to see and hear meaning? There are six such principles or rules of perception. They represent the conclusions of a movement in psychology called "the Gestalt School." Although the Gestalt movement itself does not have the same following it once had, its principles of perception have endured. These perception programs lead us to perceive things as whole, continuous forms rather than as disjointed light or sound.[4]

Proximity

Look at the lines in Figure 5.2. The lines in the "A" group seem to make four two-dimensional columns. By simply moving the lines into a new proximity, the "B" group seems to be three two-dimensional columns with two outside lines unrelated to the others. The only difference between "A" and "B" is the relative proximity of the lines. Because some lines are closer than others, we arrange them into different patterns in our minds. The principle is a simple one: **Elements close together tend to be perceived as a unit.** This is the first of the gestalt principles. It is more like a program of perception than a principle. It is a program that leads us to assume relatedness when things are seen relatively close to each other. When our ancestors first gazed at the stars, it was this program that led them to assume the meaning in the stars' relative positions. The program is essential for our survival. We use it to comprehend the meaning of a double line on a highway, to grasp the meaning of signs and symbols, and it is essential for reading.

- - - - - -

Action:
Readthislineasfastasyoucanwithoutthehelpofaguidingfinger. Youwill
discoverthatitisdifficultbecausetherearefewnaturalchangesinproximity
tohelpyouidentifytheindividualwords.Nowreadthenextlineswiththe
groupingsmadevisiblebyachangeintheproximityofthewordstoeachother.

**Read this line as fast as you can without the help of a guiding finger.
You will discover that it is not as difficult because there are natural
changes in word proximity to help you identify the individual words.
These lines are quickly understood because the groupings are made vis-
ible by a change in the proximity of the words to each other.**

- - - - - -

This same gestalt principle is relevant to sound perception as well. We
are able to perceive melodies because of at least three ways the notes are
grouped: 1) the "fit" of the notes into a key or chord structure, 2) differenti-
ation of the pitch of one note from another, and 3) the separation of the
notes by silences. The notes of "Mary Had A Little Lamb" make musical
sense to us in part because the notes flow in packages of notes closely related
in time. The proximity that is involved in hearing music is time proximity.
Change the intervals between the notes and the melody changes.

A delightful example of the way timing, harmonic intervals and rhythm
can hold the meaning of a set of notes can be heard in a piece written by Igor
Stravinsky. The work is called "Greeting Prelude." It contains all the notes of
the familiar "Happy Birthday To You," but the notes jump around between
two or three octaves as the dynamic range of the piece also changes. What
makes this musical joke recognizable as a variation of "Happy Birthday . . ."
is the fact that the rhythm and relative harmonic intervals of the notes is to a
large extent preserved.[5]

The concept is simple: things that seem close together in space or time
tend to be perceived as a unit.[6]

Similarity

The second gestalt principle or perception program is the principle of similarity. Look at Figure 5.3. Most people tend to see a circle with a wedge
shape accented. In fact, the illustration is of a set of short lines arranged in an
area where some are horizontal and some are perpendicular. This is an illustration of the proximity principle. The impression of the circle is created by

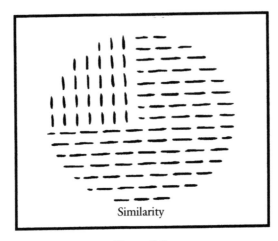

Similarity

Figure 5.3

the proximity of the lines. The wedge is suggested by making a quarter of the lines perpendicular. Their similarity leads us to see a pie shape or a "Pac-Man," if our attention is drawn to the bigger part of the "circle." We tend to group like objects together. It is true of the things we see and it is true of the things we hear. In the case of seeing, it is this principle that enables us to discern words from the lighted bulbs on a matrix of light bulbs above a freeway. In the case of hearing, it is the principle that allows us to conclude that a series of discrete sounds and pitches have enough similarity to make them all part of a Verdi aria or a Beatles song.[7]

Good Continuation

The third principle is the principle of "good continuation." The principle of good continuation means that elements forming a familiar or "good figure" will tend to be perceived together as parts of a larger whole. Look at Figure 5.4. The limbs are assumed to cross behind the tree trunk. Our mind expects lines that we see to continue when they are out of sight Even though the limbs cannot be seen to continue and cross behind the trunk, we assume they do. A pattern has been established that is familiar: two almost straight limbs. We cannot help but perceive that the two cross because they seem to have "good continuation." The sketch next to the trunk shows that it is possible for both the limbs to turn behind the tree. If it were not for this perceptual "jumping to conclusions," we would not be able to appreciate any art or symbol. Almost any representation of the world that a person fabricates depends on the quick, unconsidered leaps of logic if it is to be recognized.

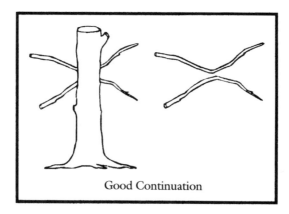

Good Continuation

Figure 5.4

We make the leap visually when we are able to appreciate a painting by Van Gogh, or when we see meaning in a diagram. In the case of Van Gogh, we do not usually perceive pigment on a flat surface, but rather a "starry night."

We make the leap musically when we are able to appreciate the several "voices" of a Bach invention. We do not usually perceive sound waves, volume and pulses of rhythm; we perceive music.[8]

Closure

The fourth principle of perception is the principle of closure. Closure means that when we see or sense part of a thing, we tend to fill in the missing detail. Ambiguity or meaninglessness is next to impossible for us to perceive. It takes a good bit of effort to look at Figure 5.5 without seeing two circles, one partially eclipsing the other. The same principle is at work when we listen to sounds in the night or with our eyes shut: we tend to fill out what we are receiving through our ears with images of things that might be seen. When we talk on the telephone, listen to a radio program or listen to a recording, we automatically fill in the missing detail. Auditory clues as to the meaning of what we are receiving are all we need to allow our brain to supply the missing visual clues that would fill out the event. We tend to foreclose on experience so that there are no "loose ends." [9]

Symmetry

The fifth principle is the principle of symmetry. To say that we tend to perceive symmetrical forms before we see asymmetrical ones is to say that we are

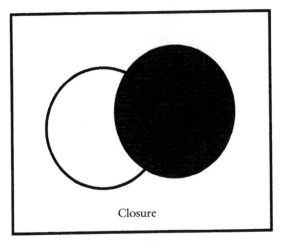

Closure

Figure 5.5

drawn to balance. There is something in the way in which we model the world that leads us to see or hear balanced and symmetrical patterns first. Look at Figure 5.6. Most who see these patterns will see triangular patterns in a box. Why don't we see a combination of "K" figures as easily? A "K" lacks the symmetry of a triangle. This principle leads us to see symmetrical patterns in nature and predisposes us to assume that symmetry is the norm in life.[10] It is the principle that allows us to appreciate the balance of a Paul Simon ballad, the structural symmetry of a willow tree, or the symmetry of an Imogene Cunningham photograph.

Figure And Ground

Finally, our perceptual programs include the principle of Figure and Ground. A whole thing is perceived when its form and pattern become meaningful (the function of the first five programs or principles of perception), and when it is located against some ground or backdrop. The well-known optic illusion in Figure 5.7 demonstrates the powerful way that the definition of an object's background defines the object. You can make yourself see either two faces in profile or a vase. It is next to impossible not to see one or the other, and it is difficult if not impossible to see both at the same time. The principle is simple: we tend to identify a background for the objects we perceive. The artwork of M. C. Escher makes imaginative use of the figure-ground principle to play with the viewer. In a painting called "Study of Regular Division of the Plane with Angel and Devils," Escher confronts us with a conglomeration of angels and devils that alternate between being figure and ground

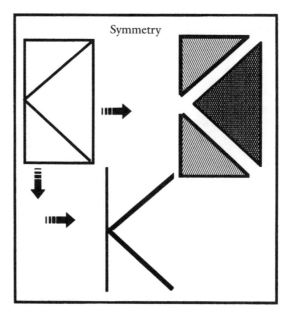

Figure 5.6

depending on what we choose as the object of our attention.[11] In the case of sounds, we are always listening to one thing that is the auditory "figure" that has a place in a larger background of noise. As we shift our attention from one sound to another, what was once a part of the background noise emerges as the sound listened to. When we listen to a melody of an orchestral piece, the melody is the "figure" and the orchestration is the "ground."

As these six programs lead our perception, we are able to perceive a whole thing. Imagine that you are looking at a series of lines, shapes, light and dark, shades, colors and masses. With these six programs leading your eyes in an investigation of the scene, you are able to "leap" to the conclusion that you are looking at four tennis balls on a box, on a shelf, in a cluttered garage. Although we cannot see all sides of the balls or the box, we have no doubt that the backs or obscured parts are there. Although we have not looked closely at the contents of the garage or at the structure of the garage itself, the few clues leave no doubt about the scene's context. Although you do not examine all the balls, you conclude that they are a set. The scene instantly is one thing—a gestalt. It is the whole thing that you can relate to and act in. Mundane as such an event is, it nevertheless demonstrates a deeply complex and wonderful event: perception.

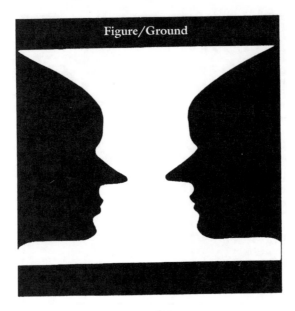

Figure 5.7

MEMORY: CHICKEN OR EGG?

The formula for the recognition of meaningful objects and sounds is incomplete with just these six "gestalt programs." The data which our brains attend to would amount to nothing unless there were a mechanism for matching sensory input with similar meaningful patterns in memory. So the missing piece in the perception formula is the content of one's memory. Memory is a catch-all concept for several kinds of storage in the cortex. Chapter Two included a diagram that depicted three kinds of memory: sensory memory (latent sound, image, taste, smell, feeling that last for a few seconds), short-term or working memory (a conscious recollection of what is just sensed or recalled that fades within a few seconds or minutes if not elaborated or "memorized"), and long-term memory (information, events, models, thoughts, feelings that are more or less permanently integrated along the neuronal pathways of the cortex that can be retrieved back into short-term or working memory).

The common element in all of them is this: each one refers to some sort of stored data that can be "called" or "hooked" into conscious or unconscious thinking operations. Whether we are aware of the memory as it is activated or not, any data or pattern that is stored in the cortex (permanently or momentarily) and is used in thinking is memory. (Almost all memory is stored in the cortex. The exception is motor skill memory that has become habitual. Many of these memory patterns are stored in the spinal cord closer to the muscles used in the action or skill.)

When I look at my garage, the shapes, lines, and shades linger long enough in my sensory "buffer" to take up "residence" in my working memory. There, if I am interested, they hook long-term memories that they resemble in key ways. These older memories serve as models for what I see. If my perceptions match my memories, I recognize the scene. If I have had no experience of garages, tennis balls or boxes, I would not be able to recognize the scene as a garage with tennis balls on a box on a shelf. A gestalt would be slow to take shape. Recognition, therefore, depends on both sensory input perceived and meaningful models that the data "hooks" and matches. The memories can be as specific as "garage" or "ball" and as nonspecific as "curve" or "corner."

Memory is so important to the task of perception that it is easy for an expectation to overwhelm the perception process and lead us to ignore what our eyes or ears receive. We jump to conclusions because the stored expectation is so strong. Examples range from the innocuous (a child clinging to a stranger's leg in a crowd, thinking it is dad's) to the tragic (a frightened homeowner shooting a family member thought to be an intruder).

If memory is so important to the process of perception, how is it possible for a person to ever recognize a thing? Don't we come into life with a relatively empty cortex? Remember that the primary function of the cortex is to find patterns and affix meaning to them. This is the modeling function of the brain. As we began our lives, we fixed feeling tones and pleasure-pain valences to experiences of sight, sound, and touch. When certain experiences tended to be pleasant and fulfilled needs, they were stored as pleasant memories. These memories then helped us to perceive subsequent similar experiences more completely. What came first, then, were the programs of perception and the overriding drive to find patterns. As we grew through childhood, the memories took a greater role in the perception process. For some, memory becomes so strong that it is hard to see a new thing. For others, memory is doubted to a degree that they seem to be surrounded by chaos. But for most of us our growth into adulthood has been accompanied by an increased dependence on stored models to fill out our incomplete perceptions. However, from time to time we are rudely reminded of the limited nature of our stereotypical models and are led to take a fresh (childlike) look at our world.

I SEE!

There is a popular optic illusion that seems to be a series of random black and white patches. The illusion is meant to be ambiguous and gives no clue as to what is the figure and ground. The caption says, "What is this?" (see Figure 5.8). The question implies that we ought to be able to see a figure in the picture. The problem is that most of the clues carried by shades of gray, broken lines, and patterns are missing. I can remember the first time that I saw the illusion: I could not force a meaningful perception out of the light and dark shapes. They were only shapes on a white piece of paper. Even as I was coached with clues by a teacher, the mystery of the picture only frustrated me. I was told that it was a picture of a dog, a spotted dog, and even of a spotted dog in a wooded setting, but the picture was still meaningless.[12]

It was not until after another student outlined the dog with his finger did the animal nearly leap from the picture. In a moment, when the legs of the dog were traced, it all came together. It was as if the dog wasn't there before I saw it. Then when I saw it, it appeared. I cannot NOT see the dog when I see that picture now and have a hard time understanding how someone else cannot see it.

What I want to emphasize with this illustration is that the programs of perception and the hooking of meaningful memory to turn sensory data into meaning HAPPENS IN A MOMENT. It is the "A-HA moment" as the gestalt psychologists would call it (notably Wolfgang Kohler).[13] It happens in a flash when line, pattern, shade, memory and environment fall into place to

Figure 5.8

"reveal" a thing in time and place. The recognition or meaning happens as a gestalt. I don't mean to say that the programs of perception work all at once (maybe they do, maybe they don't); rather, I mean to say that the combining of the pieces of the puzzle reveals something meaningful in a moment of revelation. Further, I want to suggest that the same process of revelation happens at *each* of the Ten Levels of Meaning described in Chapter Two. Whether we perceive a shape, a feeling, a value, or a religious concept, there is a moment when we "see" the thing or idea in a moment of perception. At each successive level of meaning, the import and scope of the perception is more expansive. Yet each level of perception employs essentially the same set of processes involving the basic perception programs used to identify a voice or a doorknob.

Consider this: now and then there are things or events that our minds decipher at many or all the levels of meaning at once. Such "A-HA moments" are like explosions within us that leave us shaken and sometimes transformed. The fuse or blasting cap of the explosive stick of meaning is raw data that our senses take in, classify, recognize, and locate. Then its being "explodes" through our meta-physical models of the world with upsetting force. It shakes our identity, stretches and snaps relationships, calls into question what we think is right, scrambles our conception of history—not to mention our destiny—and threatens to tear our cosmos apart. These explosions can vary in intensity and thoroughness and so there are several kinds:

The Emmaus Walk Explosion: In the Gospels of Luke and Mark, there is the account of two Jesus followers conversing about the death and resurrection reports of their rabbi. They are joined by the alive-again Jesus and walk with him till dark without recognizing him. It is not until they sit and break bread together that the two, in a sudden explosion of meaning, recognize Jesus. Without trying to do the job of biblical criticism, I want to use the story as a model of one kind of "A-HA moment"—one where a strong experience forces a reworking of very strong assumptions. The recognition of Jesus came from the combining of their sensory cues with the memory of the saving activity of God in Hebrew history, plus their experiences with Jesus prior to his death. The event exploded as a life-changing "A-HA." The person so central to their lives had been gone, and now he was back. Have you had similar explosive experiences? Experiences of a person or situation that could not fit into your model of the world but could not be denied? An experience so strong that it rearranged your self, your values and your cosmos?

The Helen Keller Explosion: Thanks to the two brilliant film versions of the story of the education of Helen Keller, her journey from a world of chaos to a world of meaning is a part of our common culture. It can serve to illustrate another example of the "explosive A-HA." On that explosive occasion when Helen's hands felt water in a way that it became once and for all associated with the hand sign for water and the vocalization of the word, her world's pieces fell into a shape that never had been before. Because of the efforts of Annie Sullivan to teach a vocabulary for the blind and deaf Keller, and then to train her hands to be her "tele-sensors," the moment came when the "vocabulary" began to match what her hands "saw" and "heard." The event was a life-changing "A-HA."[14] Have you had similar experiences when a final bit of a puzzle served to reveal the whole picture? When a concept finally became sharp with one more experience or piece of data?

The Falling Apple Explosion: Another variation on the "A-HA moment" is pointed to by the legend of how Isaac Newton came to conceive of the nature of gravitation. As Isaac sat beneath an apple tree, a falling apple struck him on the head. The event, as the story goes, led him to make a conceptual leap about the reason objects fall: there must be a force of attraction that is equal to all objects! This moment of revelation is similar to the others, but in this case it has to do with a commonplace physical event making an unexpected impression on our models of the physical world. The impression was of such significant meaning that it brought new understanding.

Whether explosive moments or quiet awakenings, these epiphanies are the building materials for the development of a person's world of meaning. The next chapter will look at a **pedagogy of perception** that is intended to guide us further in our tasks as religious educators.

CHAPTER SIX

A Pedagogy of Perception

CONSIDER this proposition:

IF we fashion the models of the physical world according to the gestalt principles,

AND IF our meta-physical models are built in the same manner,

THEN we can help others to be intentional about building models of the meta-physical world, as we assist them to use the gestalt principles as guiding questions for parsing and constructing meaning from experience.

Here are the guiding questions stated in their general form:

1. Similarity: What patterns of meaning merge when similar elements are identified and grouped?
2. Symmetry: What patterns of meaning emerge when contrasting, balancing, and paradoxical elements are identified and grouped?
3. Closure: What patterns seem to be whole and complete?
4. Good continuation: What patterns of meaning seem to be suggested by present trends or patterns?
5. Proximity: What patterns of meaning emerge when elements that are closely related in space and time are identified and grouped?
6. Figure/ground: What patterns of meaning seem to be emerging as figure (object, form) and what is their meaningful ground?

Since these ways of thinking and perceiving are already part of the natural thought processes, I suggest that if they are applied intentionally and critically to our pursuit of meaning, the pursuit will be more fruitful.

Yet, the questions must be employed with caution. They are based on the perception protocols of our brains, not scientific method. They are hunchmakers, not proof developers. I don't mean to say that we are naturally illogical, because we are not. Rather, perception and problem-solving programs of the brain allow us to quickly identify our immediate situation and then make decisions in the shortest time. We are set for speed rather than for accuracy, so it is incumbent upon educators to help students bring these

71

hunchmakers to consciousness, and to encourage students to always beware of jumping to conclusions and being fooled by too little information. Our natural tendency is to build meaning rather than to analyze components. Critical thinking is, however, an important part of the strengthening of our models of the meta-physical world. The six guiding questions have six companion caution questions that serve to guide the parsing of meaning:

1. Similarity: Just because two events have similar elements doesn't guarantee that they carry the same meaning. So the following questions ought always to be on our minds as we help students to build their metaphysical models: Are the elements that I see as similar basically so, or is the similarity only superficial? Have I missed some basic dissimilarity that negates my assumptions?

2. Symmetry: Sometimes what has outward balance or symmetry is unrelated after a closer look. Whether it be two people who look alike or two events that have similar components, what is deeper may have little symmetry or balance. The following questions are aimed at addressing this real possibility: Is the symmetry, balance or contrast artificial? Am I using some memory of past experience to force the appearance of balance and symmetry?

3. Closure: Often when events or ideas seem complete, we find that there's much more to be said or developed. The following questions keep this possibility in mind: Have I "filled in" missing pieces to my perception too soon? Have I made leaps of logic and assumptions that are unfounded?

4. Good Continuation: How often are we fooled by a picture or optic illusion that makes us think that some object is longer, or extended, when it is not? The same error can happen when we think of history, identity, and the like. The following questions keep this error in mind: Are my assumptions about patterns warranted? Am I led by other kinds of evidence than just continuation?

5. Proximity: We expect things, people, ideas, and events that are close in space and time to be related. But we can be fooled. The following questions are meant to keep students' minds on this possibility: Is it possible that events that happen close to each other in time are unrelated? Have I mistakenly connected ideas or meanings just because they seem to come up together?

6. Figure/Ground: One of the most common optical errors is a figure-ground confusion. It is so easy to mistake the shape of an object if the background is not obvious. So it is also with ideas and meanings. If we misunderstand the context of an idea, the idea is liable to be garbled. The following questions point to this kind of error: Can there be another context for this idea? Do I have a good idea of what the nature of the context or larger picture of a concept?

Table 6.1a
QUESTIONS GENERATED AT THE INTERSECTIONS OF THE PROTOCOLS OF PERCEPTION AND THE SIX CIRCLES OF META-PHYSICAL MEANING

SIMILARITY
What patterns of meaning emerge when similar elements are grouped?

IDENTITY	COMMUNITY	VALUES
Whose, who, what am I? What similarities exist in the episodes of my life story and what meaning do they reveal?	**How am I linked to others?** What similarities do I experience in my relationships with others? Are there relationships themes revealed in my friendships and kinships?	**What is important?** Are there similarities in the ways human conduct effects the common good and social fabric? Do those patterns suggest principles for social action
HISTORY **Why do things happen?** Are there similarities in past events that reveal in their likenesses causes for history?	**FUTURE** **What is going to happen?** We project insights of the past as forecasts and hopes for time to come. Are there similarities to these predictions? What common elements are there in various predictions? future?	**COSMOS** **What is at the heart of things?** Are there similarities in the way the physical world works? Do these similarities reveal patterns about forces that are at work in creation?

SYMMETRY
What patterns of meaning emerge when contrasting, balancing and paradoxical elements are identified and grouped?

IDENTITY	COMMUNITY	VALUES
Does my life story reveal a balance, contrast or paradox of attitudes, focus or purpose? When do they mean? What meaning emerges when I compare balancing or contradictory motifs of my life?	What is revealed about human community when I examine the people and groups I choose to identify as "Them" or "Us," "Friend" or "Foe"? What do my hierarchies of power mean?	What patterns emerge when contrasting and opposing principles of social action, aesthetics and mores "compete" for my fidelity? Is there more to ethical/aesthetic symmetry than right/wrong, beauty/ugly?
HISTORY What patterns of meaning emerge when opposing or balancing historical trends are juxtaposed? Are there forces at work in the shaping of events that reveal balance and pattern?	**FUTURE** We cannot speak of the lessons of the future, but we can project the lessons of the past so as to help us envision the future. What are the opposing and balancing forces that we expect will shape the time to come?	**COSMOS** Does there seem to be a balance and symmetry to the operation of the cosmos and do those patterns reveal meaning?

Table 6.1b
QUESTIONS GENERATED AT THE INTERSECTIONS OF THE PROTOCOLS OF PERCEPTION AND THE SIX CIRCLES OF META-PHYSICAL MEANING

PROXIMITY

What patterns of meaning emerge when elements that are close together in space and time are identified and grouped?

IDENTITY	COMMUNITY	VALUES
What do I mean by the possessions I keep close to me? What meaning is behind actions I do in the space of a short time?	What do I mean by the relationships I keep and the people I stay close to? Does my "Web of Group Affiliations" reveal a pattern of meaning? Is there a spiritual ecology at work in my here-and-now communities?	Does proximity and contemporaneity play in the values I choose or the way I define beauty? When they are out of sight are they out of mind?

HISTORY	FUTURE	COSMOS
What truth emerges when events that happen close in time and space are examined?	To what degree is the "past prologue"? Must the future evolve from those events that just occurred, or can there be surprises?	What truth can be discovered when we look at the clusters of natural phenomenon and how they work? Does the principle of "ecology" mean something?

CLOSURE

Are there patterns that seem to be whole and complete, ones that are finished?

IDENTITY	COMMUNITY	VALUES
Are there attitudes, skills and self-understandings that seem completed or whole in my psyche? Do I have a sense of my own wholeness? What parts of my self have I closed off or declared finished too soon?	Do I have friendships or kinships that are so complete as to withstand trauma, conflict and separation? Have I closed my circle of relationships so as to preclude others?	Are there unifying principles of right behavior and aesthetics that gives my life a well-rounded quality?

HISTORY	FUTURE	COSMOS
Is there some unifying integrity, force or factor at work in history that is revealed at least partially in every event? Are there ages and epochs that have run their course allowing a new age to begin?	Is there a plan for the future? Can there be a completion or closure to the themes of history? Will time ever come to an end?	Of what about the cosmos can we be sure Do we know enough about creation to make conclusions about its origin and destiny?

Table 6.1c
QUESTIONS GENERATED AT THE INTERSECTIONS OF THE PROTOCOLS OF PERCEPTION AND THE SIX CIRCLES OF META-PHYSICAL MEANING

GOOD CONTINUATION

What patterns of meaning seem to be suggested by trends or present experience? What can we "take on faith" from what we see, experience?

IDENTITY	COMMUNITY	VALUES
What do I seem to be making of myself? Where am I going? What will I be?	Given the incomplete knowledge we have of others with whom we are related, can I trust others? Can I place my faith in others to stay related to me?	What are the consequences if the aesthetic or ethical climate continues? Ought the values of the present be continued into the future?
HISTORY	**FUTURE**	**COSMOS**
What is likely to continue to happen in the human drama?	What trends of the present will likely contribute to what happens next?	What patterns of meaning seem to be hinted at with our present knowledge of the cosmos? Do we have enough of the puzzle of creation to at least point to its origins and directions, its creator and sustainer?

FIGURE AND GROUND

What patterns of meaning seem to be FIGURE (subject, object or content) and which seem to be GROUND (background, frame, context)?

IDENTITY	COMMUNITY	VALUES
What is the nature of the world around me, the stage upon which I grow? Do I stand out from the world in some particular way? How do I contribute to the physical and meta-physical ground upon which I exist?	Who am I as a family member and friend? Do my relationships serve as background for me or do the relationships take center stage with me as prop? How does my ethnicity function in the play of figure and ground?	What is the figure/ground relationship of good/evil, beauty/ugly? Is there an ethical and aesthetic background that is better for human life than others?
HISTORY	**FUTURE**	**COSMOS**
Events can be figure and ground. Over the sweep of history, who or what seems to be figure (the main action or central actor), and what seems to be context or staging?	What forces, principles or influences seem to remain solid as the future unfolds? Is there some ethical or aesthetic "ground" that will best nurture and support life in the future?	What is the meaning and nature of creation and how do I fit in it? Does it have integrity? Can I define it or does it define me? How do I commune and relate to what is at the heart of the cosmos?

Table 6.1 is a grid interlacing the gestalt principles with the six metaphysical levels of meaning (see Figure 6.1). The grid has been filled out with the questions each intersection generates. When I first filled out the grid, two ideas took shape. One idea was that the questions have the look of a catechism. They are, in fact, the essential theological and philosophical questions, the answers to which comprise one's credo. The second idea had to do with the environment within which these questions get answered or changed. It was just after the nuclear accident in Chernobyl that I finished the grid. I had just watched the report on television. One of the segments of the broadcast emphasized the power of skillfully and sensitively led dialogue to help persons answer these questions on meaning.

A news commentator was reporting from a junior high school, getting impressions from members of a social studies class. The teacher was encouraging the students to express their thoughts and feelings about the accident. The members of the class were sharing their opinions about the cause of the accident, about the differences between U.S. nuclear technology and that of the Russians, and the like.

Finally the teacher asked, "What do you think it all means?" Several expressed their fears, and some admitted that it was too far away for them to really worry about. Then one student said, "I think the Russians got exactly what they deserved." Immediately another student spoke up: "It didn't happen to Russians; it happened to people! Just because we might not like the Russian government doesn't mean that bad things ought to happen to them."

The class was silent for a moment. The teacher asked if the students could imagine what it was like for the families who lived near the accident. Many said they could and shared their thoughts. The commentator concluded with thoughts about empathy and compassion and the news switched to something else.

The report came back to me as I looked at the grid. The students of the class were being helped by the teacher and each other to deal with several levels of meaning as the accident was discussed. They were talking about values, identity, history, and the future. In their conversations they dealt with perceptions of the news event and of the people of Russia. In the mix of sharing, listening and arguing, they were helping each other to avoid some of the errors of perception to which we are all prone. It was in the give-and-take of the group that this clarification took place.

It is in the context of free and trusting conversation in which a variety of perceptions can be exchanged that one's metaphysical world is best clarified. It is even better if the conversation is led by someone who is committed to the process and sensitive to its dynamics. In the process, critical thinking gets done. How it is encouraged with young children will be different from how it is done with teens or adults, but every age can be led to think reflectively and critically. At the heart of the process is a climate of trust and freedom which gets initiated by asking and encouraging questions.

I am saying that the perception protocols, so essential to organizing the physical world, are also in operation as we organize our metaphysical world. The more we let these protocols inform our plans for religious education, the more effective our efforts will be.

WORSHIP: THE POWER
OF FIGURE AND GROUND

I believe that the most productive of the perception protocols, in terms of generating fresh thinking about religious education and nurture, is the protocol involved in identifying figure and ground.

Consider the experience of worship as a case of the centrality of figure-ground. Lately religious educators have returned to the conviction that participation in the regular celebrations of the faith community is among the most powerful shapers of meaning and culture.[1] Let's see how this experience of worship is such a potent shaper of religious being.

The anthropologist describes worship as that peculiar human activity within which the gathered community of believers rehearse and remember the formative stories, meanings and liturgies of their culture.[2] Worship puts the worshiper in closer communion with the object and source of faith, life and health.

Paul Tillich described the worship experience and religious experience in general as experiences involving one's Ultimate Concern.[3] The object of a person's ultimate concern is that person's Ground of Being: God. Worship, then, is that event wherein a person fixes his or her being or identity on a background that has God, or "Ultimacy," as its primary texture, depth, and color. Using this analogy, then, another way of defining one's God is to use words that define the central unifying element of one's meta-physical models of the world. Such words and symbols are the content and environment of worship.

So consider the worshiper and the worship event. It is very much like the circus experience described in the second chapter. As the believer enters the place of worship, expectations and memories are hooked and "reeled" into consciousness. The combination of the nature of the morning, the routines of preparation, the sights and smells of the place of worship—all serve to bring forth models and put them into our working memory. From the point of view of the worshiper, worship is the experience of stepping out of the ordinary context of life into the sacred context. Colors, symbols, sounds, textures, spaces and other elements serve to form a ground or context against which a person can live, move, and have being. Worship is the ground, the worshiper is the figure. Or, to put it in terms of the levels of modeling discussed in the last chapter, our identity model is the figure, and other meta-physical models, as they are represented in the sensations of worship, and serve as the background upon which we take shape. It can be an extremely powerful combination of figure and ground.

Worship is not the only time and place that is so powerfully a ground to our identities. Any institutional environment can be ground to us. In fact, *any* environment to some degree redefines us as we move against its background. The uniqueness of the worship environment is that it is one we choose and one that has as its unifying principle the subject of our model of the cosmos. A major league baseball game may be rich with symbols, ritual, music, myths, stories and passion, but most people do not step into the stadium with a sense that they are going to commune with what is at the heart of the universe. A ballgame is, however, exactly like worship in that it is a powerful ground for who I am when I go to the game. Both the ballgame and worship hook a set of behaviors and values that some other environment does not address. They call out of me a way of being and acting that can be overwhelming.

The persons who create worship experiences are artists, "painting" backgrounds on the canvas of a sanctuary, a gathering, a meeting house, or even out-of-doors. Using a palate of music, movement, words, colors, clothing, stories and prayers, the worship artist paints a context upon which each worshiper becomes a figure. The persons who step into that context to worship come there expecting that the experience will form a familiar "picture" which will illuminate, nurture, challenge and highlight their identity in a familiar way.

Worship can do or cause one or some combination of the following four things: 1) it can confirm and nurture one's identity and self-understanding; 2) it can challenge, disturb, or change one's self-understanding; 3) it can fail to create a clear enough ground to affect one's self-understanding; 4) it can confuse and disintegrate one's self-understanding.

For the most part, worship tends to accomplish the first of these four. After all, people do not continue to place themselves into a context that seems destructive or abrasive to who they are unless they have no choice. Nor do people continue to place themselves into a context that has no relevance to who they are if it is their choice. I suggest that the decline in worship attendance among mainline moderate and liberal Protestant congregations has much to do with the fact that worship is either confusing and negative to them, or that it makes no difference at all.

Similarly, the congregations that are growing are creating a worship context that either confirms and excites the self-understanding of the worshipers in a positive way, or helps them to rebuild a shattered self-understanding.

I don't mean to say that "how the worship will play" ought to be the first consideration in the design of worship. The first consideration ought to be the requirements of the faith. But the second consideration must be the way the worship acts as both redemptive and nurturing background to the participants. Too often, worship-designers create a context that will "sell" without regard to the depth of the faith it is supposed to communicate. To use Harvey Cox's term, worship of that variety is merely a "seduction of the spirit."[4]

Instead of the example of worship, we could just as easily apply the power of figure-ground to a classroom experience, camping, backpacking, or a committee meeting. Each of them is ground to our figures, our selves. Each exerts a power that is considerable and cumulative.

Because of the power of a context or ground (such as worship or an educational event) to form, inform and transform one's identity model, care and thought must be given to the process. In the case of Christian worship, the first step is for the creator of the event to place himself or herself onto the ground of meaning that is the gospel. Likewise in Jewish worship, the rabbi must begin by putting himself or herself on the ground and meaning that is Torah. By doing so, the worship-creator allows the meta-physical meanings of the faith community to bring out the self-understanding most consistent with that community. Only after the worship-planner has been reoriented to this source should the work of creation for congregational worship begin. It is no different for the teacher creating a religious educational experience.

We come to know who and whose we are in the context of a bigger picture. Worship, education and community life are not the only "grounds" against which people take shape, but they are among the most potent of these big pictures. They are effective arenas wherein people form faithful models of the world. They are redemptive places for pilgrims seeking answers to the puzzle of life. To what degree do we encourage faith pilgrims to address the meaning questions I have outlined? Does our classroom curricula encourage the search? Does worship celebrate the questions and answers?

SUMMARY

Lying on one's back outdoors late on a clear night isn't usually an occasion to reflect on the mechanisms of cognition and perception. More often than not, it is an occasion for romance, wonder, philosophizing, questioning, or just relaxing. As our brains go about their relentless task of finding patterns and meaning hidden in the stars' proximity, similarity, and all the rest, what we perceive up there is the universe stretching out beyond imagination. There are times when we have been so aware of the size and scope of it all that the great canvas of the universe has served to redefine our very being. We sense a whole sky full of star patterns as well as universal meanings almost too large to take in. Such flights of intellect, spirit and emotion are possible because of these mechanisms of perception. They are like doors that let the whole universe pour in and like a factory that re-forms it all into the miniature universe we carry around in the synapses of our brains.

CHAPTER SEVEN

Metaphor and Understanding

INSIGHT AND METAPHOR

UNDERSTANDING is achieved through **struggle**. It is gained when the seeker braves some **chaos, armed** with proven meanings, a willingness to embrace the confusion, and the patience to discover a metaphor for its inner pattern.

Consider this example of a struggle to understand: Michael has an active mind and a playful imagination. He likes to know and understand. He does not like not knowing. Not to know is uncomfortable for him. I usually know when Michael is uncomfortable or bewildered over an idea. He will **bite** into a confusion like a **bulldog with lockjaw**. Not angrily, mind you, but with intense interest and determination to **taste** a mystery and know its secret.

I was teaching a Sunday school class that had children ranging from first to sixth grade. Michael had just finished fourth grade. Our class was a summer-long learning lab centered on the theme of God's good creation and our partnership with God to care for it. There were learning centers around the room that encouraged discovery about the world through several simple science experiments and art or learning projects. Michael liked to learn about the planets, magnets and motors.

On one occasion we began the class with a prayer. Several children contributed by thanking God for their pets, family and life. One child prayed that God might make her cat well (it had been injured in a fight). After the prayer, I noticed Michael had that **bulldog** look about him. He went to the library shelf and looked up something in the dictionary, went to the Bible search table and found a passage he wanted, then sat back down.

Near the end of the class he was still sitting. I sat with him and asked what was on his mind.

"I don't get it!" His voice was **raised**. "God has laws. You get in the way [of them] and you can get hurt, like April's cat. Why should God fix her cat? I had a dog that got run over! He died. If I had prayed, would God stop the world and fix him? My mom said that accidents just happen and God is sad when they happen, but he can't change the rules every time a bad accident happens. If that cat gets cured, I'm gonna be mad! I like to pray, but I didn't think it was supposed to be magic. And if it is, does God only care about the things that we pray about? Mom says praying **isn't** like a **Santa list.**"

I listened a few minutes (Michael doesn't have trouble expressing himself). Then I asked him what he had found when he looked in the books earlier. "The dictionary said prayer was an 'earnest request.' Mom says it is talking to God. When I pray, I tell God what's up, you know, what's on my mind. Sometimes I tell him I am glad, or scared, or mad. I ask for his advice and stuff, but I don't beg. The Bible **passage** you showed us was about Moses arguing with God in that tent. This is confusing." The class was over and we agreed to talk more about his confusion at a later time.

The next week at prayer time April thanked God for her cat getting better and Michael sat silent as she told about the trip to the vet and the bandages on her cat's leg. When April finished telling her story, Michael simply said, "It was the vet." He still had the **bulldog** look as he went to the magnet center.

About five minutes later I heard a **yelp** from among the magnets and Michael called me urgently.

"Look here!" He was wide-eyed. Michael shook some iron filings out on a sheet of construction paper. "A **mess**," he said pointing at the black shavings. Then from underneath he brought a magnet up against the paper. The shavings shifted into the pattern of the lines of the magnet's magnetic field. "All together!" The **bulldog** was gone. In its place was a pint-sized Moses after an encounter with the **burning bush.** I was still **in the dark** about what he saw on that paper. "What does it mean Michael," I asked?

"I am the iron filings. The magnet is God. When I pray, I bring my **messy** thoughts into God's magnetism. I share them, I share *me,* and the more I talk the more I get straightened out, and the more. . . ." His insight still did not have words to carry it. "**Harmony?**" I suggested. "Yes, and **shape**, and I feel like *me!*" he affirmed. "**God is my magnet!**"

"What about April's cat and your dog," I asked?

"The vet and the car," he said. "The vet healed the cat and the car killed my dog. I'll talk it over with God and let you know," he teased. The cured cat and dead dog were not the problem any more. Michael had discovered prayer for himself.

Again, understanding is achieved through struggle. It is gained when the seeker braves some chaos armed with proven meanings, a willingness to embrace the confusion, and the patience to discover a metaphor's inner pattern. Michael understood.

METAPHORING

At the **heart** of the understanding process is this thinking strategy: the compulsion to compare, contrast, and make metaphorical connections between what we are familiar with and what we seek to understand That was what happened to Michael. It happens to all of us as we learn and comprehend. The patterns and meanings we already know serve to **trace an outline** around a new experience making it accessible to our world of meaning. Call it "metaphoring." It is a cognitive program that **kicks** in as soon as we begin to receive the world sensually at birth. It serves us all our lives, making conceptual learning and modeling possible.[1] It happens like this:

Imagine that you are a child that has never experienced a dog. You have stuffed animals called Bear, Beauty (a horse) and George (a monkey), but you have had no experience of a living, wiggling, jumping dog.

Then, one day you are made a present of a puppy, a real one. Your brain **takes in** the phenomenon, "looking" for a memory that can be attached to it. The puppy is the size of the stuffed animals you have. It has the color of the monkey, the eyes of the bear, and the coat of the horse. It has four legs and a tail. Perhaps it is one of these. But it moves by itself, like you do! It makes its own sounds, eats, makes messes, licks and can bite. What is it?

You are told that this stuffed animal is a dog. You then are requested to give it a name. Like so many pet names (Sergeant, Happy, Spike, Killer, Fluff), a metaphor is chosen to define the pet. When you jump, run, make noise and messes, your parents call you "Little Dickens." This quality seems to be at the **heart** of this dog, so it becomes "Dickens." You are the metaphor for the dog. The other stuffed animals participate in the identification of the pet as well. Dickens belongs to the class of "pets" to which the stuffed animals belong.

The new experience is understood as it is identified as being LIKE something already in memory. As you grow older, Dickens will serve as a metaphor for new experiences. What the dog is to you was built on memory and will become a new **building block** for future understanding.

So natural and ever-present is our urge to make metaphorical connections that we can do it with things that are, on the **surface**, nonsense.[2] For instance, look at Figure 7.1. Which shape looks like "*Maluma*" and which looks like "*Tukatee?*" Almost everyone asked connects "A" with "Maluma" and "B" with "Tukatee." The sounds are metaphors for the shapes and vice versa.

This is a powerful cognitive strategy. We seem to be born with it already in place. I call it "Metaphoring" because of the comparing/contrasting that

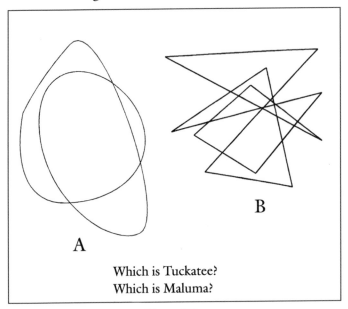

Which is Tuckatee?
Which is Maluma?

Figure 7.1

is at the center of the process. When a word or description is exactly like a new experience, it is a definition or **an equality** (e.g., human death is the irreversible secession of all brain functions), **not a metaphor**. But when this new experience is almost like a memory but on a different scale, it is the metaphorical connection we can call an analogy (death is the "big sleep"). When this experience or idea shares similar qualities but is different in obvious ways, it is a metaphorical connection we can call an allegory, figure, image, parable, or symbol (death is but "the quenching of a flame").

The word *metaphor* comes from two Greek words: *meta* (meaning: with, over, beyond, on top of—and about a dozen other spatial ideas), and *pherein* (meaning: to carry). Literally it means to be carried over or on top of. (As with so many of our words, it is a metaphor of a concrete activity applied to an abstraction.)

We constantly use physical metaphors to build ideas which are not physical. For me to say to my daughter "you are my sunshine" is to join my experience of Sarah with the experience of sunlight. I have **packaged** my experience and memory of her into a single name: Sarah. I then affirm something of what she means to me by comparing her to sunshine. The comparison and joining make it simple for me to use aspects of the physical, experiential world to **illuminate** the meaning of the meta-physical world. In fact, most (maybe all) of our analogies and metaphors find their beginning in physical experience and link the physical world with the meta-physical.

We humans can't help but make such comparisons that attach the world of ideas with things that can be experienced with the senses. Our language is **strewn** with examples: An unsophisticated, innocent young person is "not **dry behind the ears**." If two people seem to like each other and get along well together, they are said to "**cotton to each other**." A person who seems to discourage joy and celebration in others by his or her presence is thought of as a "**wet blanket**."

Sometimes the metaphor may originate from a time too far removed from our present experience and the connection gets **fuzzy**, but the meaning remains. I like this one:

> "Three sheets to the wind." This means, of course, falling down drunk, reeling from too much indulgence in strong drink, somewhat more tipsy than "half-seas over." Like many other common expressions, the phrase dates back to the times when ocean navigation was entirely by sail. But in nautical use, a sheet is not a sail, as landsmen are accustomed to suppose, but the rope or chain attached to the lower corner of a sail by which the angle of the sail is controlled. In a strong wind the sheet may be loosened and is then said to be "in the wind," flapping and fluttering without restraint. If all three sheets are loose, as in a gale, the vessel staggers and reels very much like a drunken person.[3]

In each of these examples, a more abstract or elusive idea is made accessible with the help of a comparison with familiar, **concrete** experience. Look back over this chapter at the boldface words. Literally, and by themselves, those words usually refer to something concrete. In the context of the ideas of the paragraphs, they serve to bring meaning to a concept, or depth to an experience. We cannot communicate or understand without the help of metaphors.

With a few simple experiences serving as building blocks and with rudimentary strategies for seeking and storing meaning serving as mortar, each new person begins to build great structures of meaning at birth. The perceptions and sensations of every moment recorded in the brain of an infant are like bricks stacked and cemented one on another to form names, descriptions, categories, ideas and models. These meaning structures first refer to concrete things and experiences. As the child experiences more and builds a more complex model of the world, he or she uses these words to describe more intangible experiences. It is a developmental process well documented by behavioral scientists such as Jean Piaget and linguists such as Julian

Jaynes. The process is more like building a pyramid as opposed to paving a road. The structures of meanings are cumulative.

THE POWER OF METAPHOR

So what? What difference does it make for us to know of this process of meaning-making? Simply this: If we are about the task of assisting others in the building of ideas and meanings that model God's creation, then let us do it in concert with what each of us does naturally when we think and understand. After all, this metaphoring process is powerful. Let us tap into that power.

Metaphorical thinking is powerful in at least the following ways:

1. Metaphors and analogies clarify and illuminate chaotic experiences.
2. They are powerful tools for communicating experiences to people who do not know what we know.
3. They serve to direct attention and rearrange value.
4. They can effect physical and psychological health.
5. They can help put experiences into perspective.
6. Metaphors facilitate cognitive leaps, creative insight and intellectual growth.
7. They gather and "chunk" lots of information or an unwieldy experience into a whole that is more easily remembered and used.
8. They are meaning building blocks that can stand in for full and "complete" knowledge until the fuller knowledge is discerned.

Consider each of these in turn along with some teaching-learning implications for religious education.

Metaphors and analogies clarify and illuminate chaotic experiences.
Michael pushed back some of life's chaos with his newfound metaphor. The magnet comparison shed eye-opening light on prayer for him. Cognitive scientists are coming to see that instead of being peripheral to problem-solving, this metaphoring strategy is at the core of thinking. We naturally think and decide based on analogy rather than formal logical operations of deduction or induction.[4] We can use logic, but we come to understand something more often by metaphoring. The natural way is for an old model or memory to give meaning to a new experience.

We naturally thrash around searching for relationships between the known and the obscure that are either qualitative ("My love is like a red, red rose"), quantitative ("More laughs than a barrel of monkeys") or a combination ("I'm feeling higher than a kite"). When we discover these parallels, something of the old helps us grasp the new. For Michael, his metaphorical discovery brought order back to his religious world.

Order-making metaphors do not have to be words or memories, nor do they have to be parallels that can be easily described. They may happen as unutterable "resonances" from art, music, nature, or from who knows where. I offer this personal example:

My father died in the fall of 1992. After years of heart trouble, smoking and alcoholism, his old body just quit. I had grown closer to him in the last years of his life since he had gotten sober and had begun to help so many others into the twelve-step program of Alcoholics Anonymous. At the funeral, though, I was detached. I didn't feel much of anything except annoyance at all the euphemisms and cliched expressions of sympathy. Actually, I think I was just a bit angry. Angry and what else, I didn't know. Now and then someone's authentic expression of sadness and loss would get to me, but mostly I was unaffected.

What I experienced after the funeral was a general sort of dis-ease and irritability at nothing or no one in particular. I was just anxious and fretful. I remember not being able to concentrate for very long at a time, and not being able to get excited or enthusiastic about anything. That was my condition for days on end.

I was traveling home from a meeting one night about two weeks after the funeral. The radio was tuned to a classical station that was playing Joaquin Rodrigo's "Concierto De Aranjuez" for guitar and orchestra. The middle movement is a slow adagio filled with the passion and simple minor tones that Andeluvian Spain generated and Rodrigo reclaimed. The plaintive music caught me unprepared. It was as though the emotional pollution that had circulated in me since my Dad's death was filtered and then purified and poured over me as if I were standing under a bucket. It was sad and sorrowful music that gathered my sorrow and me with it in a bath of tears and sadness that made me stop the car, listen and cry. The emotional chaos of the past weeks had found form and the limbo I had been in vanished as the orchestra and guitar found and called me.

That music was the metaphor for grief. This amount of grief was new to me. I needed some instruction, some clues about what it meant. I don't think words could have purified my muddle—only this music. What is grief like? It is like the adagio from Rodrigo's "Concierto De Aranjuez." What did it do for me? It cleared out my emotional chaos and allowed me to miss my Dad. I had to do some flailing and thrashing around with my confusion. I am grateful that the music was in my way and I stumbled onto its redemptive meaning.

Metaphors can reach us through all our senses, can be delivered through any medium and can touch our minds at any level.
Religious education ought to promote some form of "thrashing around" by providing three conditions for helpful learners wring religious meaning out of confusion. What I have in mind is not very neat. Actually, classrooms, groups and events that offer this metaphoring space may seem only a step or two this side of chaos. But that's all right, for the shining example of creating and shaping meaning is the first chapter of Genesis where God's expression of meaning was fashioned out of void and chaos.

We can promote the necessary thrashing around and discovery by guaranteeing that three conditions be present in a learning setting: 1) the space for discovery, 2) opportunity for reflection about those discoveries, and 3) a spiritual intersection where life concerns, religious ideas and metaphors can collide. These conditions will need to be prepared with the age and abilities of the students in mind, but each one of us, regardless of age, needs them in order to get on with meaning-making. Consider each of these conditions:

1. The **space** we provide can be anywhere. Just as the Tabernacle was pitched each time the Hebrews found a new grazing land, so do educators need that sort of mobility that allows them to pitch a class space anywhere. And when it gets pitched, we educators are the ones responsible for outfitting it with the tools, toys, texts, props, costumes, nature, crafts, media, stories, music, art, excursions and artifacts that provide rich resources for discovering metaphors. Thus we create a space for metaphorical discovery.

2. In addition to this discovery space, learners need **opportunities for reflection** wherein they can think about and test insights. I am again influenced by Dr. Ross Snyder. Although Snyder did not develop his approach to religious education from cognitive science, his insights about metaphors and conceptual learning are consistent with this approach. In a collection of his papers published by the World Council of Churches in 1961, he described an approach to youth ministry that had meaning-making and modeling at its center. The papers were collected as *The Ministry of Meaning*.[5] Dr. Snyder described three essentials to reflection and meaning-making: The Dive, Mating, and Celebration.

A "**Dive**" is a strategy that encourages a student to think about a fresh insight **alone**. For Snyder, the role of the teacher at this point is to encourage private reflection. He suggested that these dive times be occasions to write, compose, draw, sculpt, mold and construct the emerging idea so it might be physically out in front of the student as a fresh metaphor.

The second step in the reflective process Snyder calls "**Mating**." It refers to the strategy of connecting an individual's ideas and insights with those of other people. It is a group process of show, tell, and revise. The skilled teacher will encourage the kind of interaction that allows critical thought in the context of acceptance as each student reveals a newly created part of their world to others.

Finally, suggests Snyder, learners ought to have the chance to lift their metaphors, insights, commitments and unanswered questions in **celebration**. The teacher needs the skills of a priest as well as a teacher. The teacher needs to encourage students to sing, bless, and dedicate their worlds of meaning to what is at the heart of all meaning. Take a look at a sampling of reflective techniques in Table 7.1 Let it remind you of other ways of encouraging reflection.

Table 7.1

A LAUNDRY LIST OF REFLECTIVE STRATEGIES

DIVE Making Metaphors For Emerging Meaning Using:	MATE Connecting with Others' Metaphorical Expressions Through:	CELEBRATE Lifting Meaning in Corporate Ritual By:
Clay sculpting	Drama	Singing
Story Writing	Show and tell	Readings
Poetry Writing	Dance	Dance
Wood carving	Video production	Making music
Painting	Group mural	Praying
Banner making	Group banners	Banners
Photography	Any of the Dive	Drama
A journal	list done in	Choral reading
Recorded music	pairs or more	Procession
Drawing	Group book	Using the creations
Origami	Musical production	of the Dive and
Diagrams		Mate as
		components of
		the celebration

3. The third condition that can facilitate metaphorical religious thinking is the creation of a "spiritual intersection" where life concerns, religious ideas and metaphors can mix and collide. I have in mind classes, rooms, groups and experiences that brings students and their daily joys and struggles in juxtaposition with religious culture. This meta-physical intersection could become dangerous, threatening, or bewildering. Thus, it is essential that it take place within the care of redemptive community. Where grace, love and respect are the norms of relating, groups can be like hothouses for sprouting ideas and associations. In the context of such a redemptive ecology, reflection can happen unmolested by fear and authoritarianism.

Metaphors are powerful tools for communicating experiences.

Third, metaphorical thinking is powerful because the metaphors reveal to others what is on our minds. It helps us communicate. We experience life internally and privately. Yet we crave the opportunities to spread out our private worlds of meaning so our companions can know what we know. Two things make this possible: common biology and shared culture. Because groups of people share history, language, symbols, experiences, media, gestures, and the like, there is a collective world of meaning to start from. Because we share the same biology, we share an abundance of experience. But the culture and experiences we share serve only as a table upon which to spread our inner worlds. We still must constantly discover ways to make the details of our lives accessible to the ones to whom we choose to reveal ourselves.

Metaphors can be as sublime as a Japanese Haiku or as obvious as a slammed fist on a table. They can be as beautiful as a love song or as ugly as spitting. They can be pictures ("I felt as old as Whistler's Mother"), diagrams ("Follow the blue line on this map"), visual imagery, spoken or sung ("Like a Bridge over Troubled Waters"), sounds ("an explosion of laughter"), formulae ("I hear you 5X5"), smells ("The place smelled like a barn"), emotional metaphors ("angry clouds"), mathematical metaphors ("As simple as 2 + 2"), spatial metaphors ("down in the dumps"), social and role metaphors ("as close as sisters"), and so forth.

The more of culture and history we can expose ourselves and the students to, the more metaphorically literate we will be, and the more effectively we will communicate what is on our minds. It is a matter of exposure. It is a matter of offering opportunities for a student to try all sorts of metaphorical expression. Encourage students to put their budding thoughts in a picture, sculpture, diagram, a piece of music, a gesture/dance, into poetry, or in a story. Their ideas will become clearer and their ability to share them will be more effective.

Metaphors serve to direct attention and rearrange value.

Ideas, groups, institutions, and people can become so identified with a metaphor that the metaphor develops into a symbol or emblem for the idea, group, institution or person. We are surrounded by them: a country's flag, the gesture of the peace sign, a cross, the Star of David, a raised fist, a company logo, a team mascot. Usually the symbol has a metaphorical reminder in its form that calls to mind some of the meaning of the thing it represents. For example, the cross reminds the believer of the crucified and risen Christ. The cross is also a metaphor for the willingness of God to suffer even death to demonstrate love and grace. It is both an emblem and a metaphor.

Human beings have been symbolmakers for as far back as archaeologists can reach. Some of the oldest artifacts with which humanity has littered history have been emblems and tokens of faith. These faith metaphors have made it possible for us to make affirmations and declare loyalties without having to say a word. We pack into a single thing both ideas and passion. Instantly, these metaphors for family, clan, religion, nation, company, or cause communicate a culture, focus attention and are able to motivate action. With the sight of a single gesture, flag, or sculpture, a person's world of meaning is brought to mind, takes center stage and pumps our bodies with the chemistry and vitality of devotion.

The more we can communicate to students the "language" of emblems and symbols, the more we assist students to evaluate them. The more we encourage the fresh creation of symbolic metaphors for what they believe, the more deliberate and faithful will be their commitments.

Metaphors can affect physical and psychological health.

Twice a week a small group of cancer patients gathered in the parlor of a church in Westwood, California. They called their organization "We Can Do." Their philosophy was simple: to support each other in the battle to defeat their disease. One of the weapons in their arsenal for defeating cancer was "imaging." Their leader would guide the patients in meditations wherein they would imagine the cancer cells, for example, to be enemy invaders trying to destroy the body. In a typical imaging exercise they were instructed to imagine agents of the immune system, white blood cells and healthy tissue as soldiers passionate about defeating the cancers in an all-out war.

The results of this kind of daily imaging is unmistakable. From personal testimony of members of groups like "We Can Do," coupled with experimental studies of imaging, it is clear that there is a link between thinking and healing.[6] The link is not unclouded or predictable, but preliminary studies show that imaging is a hopeful tool for restoring health. Using simple metaphors can indeed affect the immune system positively.

Hope really seems to be the dynamic part of the connection between health and thinking. The metaphor is a tool which allows the patient to experience hope. Some oncologists believe the nature of the metaphor is important and so they fashion their guided metaphorical journeys to be very close to the way the immune system works.[7]

The implication is that if we want our classroom and educational events to carry the redemptive, healthy virtues of trust, hope, freedom, purpose, care, love and vitality, then the environment ought to carry the signs, stories, symbols and metaphors of those virtues.

Metaphors can help us put experiences into perspective.
When I was twelve, my family and I moved from North Carolina to California. In Arizona we stopped at Meteor Crater near Flagstaff to view the hole left by a meteor which had slammed into the desert a few thousand years ago. I was overwhelmed by its size as I looked over the lip down into the center of the half-mile-deep bowl. I will never forget it.

Two years later we returned to North Carolina for a visit by plane and flew over the crater. The pilot alerted us to it and banked our DC9 for a good view. There below, about the size of a quarter, was my awesome crater. I was *underwhelmed* and I will never forget it. My internal experience of the crater depended on the perspective from which I viewed it.

Like that crater experience, the metaphors we use to describe our world and share it with others put the experience in some sort of perspective. If I describe our place on the earth as like that of an ant in Central Park, I am implying something of the immensity of the world. But if I describe it as like that of passengers on a spaceship, I imply a perspective of altogether different proportions.

The metaphor can put an idea into a perspective.
Perspective is no small matter when it comes to the way we model the world. How many of us hold to a theology of God's transcendence because we were told so often that God was "King of Kings," "Lord of Lords," or "Master of the Universe?" Or, on the other hand, to what degree does our model of

God reflect the more intimate metaphor of "shepherd," "mother," "father," or "suffering servant?"

Both perspectives carry something of the truth of God's nature. Therefore, it is not fewer ways of describing our world of meaning that students need, but more. I am glad to have memories of the awesomeness of the Meteor Crater as well as its insignificance. Both are part of the reality of that place. Likewise, I am glad to have images of God's transcendence *and* immanence. Both are part of the reality of God. Since the metaphors we use have the power to shape perspective and meaning, let us use them liberally as a part of the learning environment while encouraging students to find their own perspectives. Let us also be careful that those perspectives do not encourage racist, sexist, or other bigoted perspectives to which humanity clings.[8] The best defense against these bigoted perspectives taking hold is exposure to many perspectives and models of persons grappling with the truth.

Metaphors facilitate cognitive leaps, creative insight and intellectual growth.

A nineteenth-century German scientist named Friedrich August Kekule von Stradonitz devoted his professional life to deciphering the molecular structure of solvents and other chemicals. He had hopes of manipulating them to synthesize other compounds. Benzene had him stumped. He could not imagine how six atoms of carbon and six atoms of hydrogen could join to make a chemical with the properties of Benzene. One dead end after another kept him from making sense of the compound. Then one evening he settled into a chair in front of a fire to relax. In a half sleep, he dreamed. Here is his account of what happened:

> I turned myself toward the fire and sank in a reverie. Atoms danced before my eyes. Long chains were firmly joined, all winding and turning with snake-like motion. Suddenly, one of the serpents caught its own tail and the ring thus formed, whirled before my eyes. I woke immediately and worked on the consequences the rest of the night.[9]

The dreamed metaphors of the snakes allowed him to make a cognitive leap that could explain how carbon could hold on to other carbons and hydrogen at the same time. Subsequent experiments proved him right and from that metaphorical insight, the field of organic chemistry developed with unprecedented speed.

Albert Einstein turned metaphoring into a strategy for imagining how the universe works. He called the strategy "*Gedanken* [thought] experiments." In one such thought experiment he imagined he was riding a train at the speed of light, passing others and asking if they could see him. Now I don't pretend to understand the intricacies of the Special Theory of Relativity, but Einstein's playful metaphorical stories of light, trains, mirrors and such opened up new ways of thinking about the universe. The result was an explosion of creative thinking and insight about curved space, black holes, the "big bang" and time travel.[10]

Philosopher Mark Johnson explained that the way a metaphor informs understanding is that the "entailments" (the necessary attributes) of the familiar half of the metaphor (what Julian Jaynes calls the "metaphier") get transferred to the new half (Jaynes calls this the "metaphrand") with all the implications of the first.[11] Take the example of the first line of the 23rd Psalm: "The Lord (metaphrand) is my shepherd (metaphier)." Shepherding and the role of the shepherd is descriptive of something essential about God. In Judeo-Christian experience, realizing this association can be a liberating leap of understanding.

These meaning associations can advance our understanding instantly. Think about Michael again. He will never again think of prayer in his old way. He reached a new intellectual level, helped by the stairway of a metaphor.

When these insights accumulate, not only does understanding jump ahead, but the way one thinks grows as well. Piaget's description of the way people develop cognitively is consistent with this pyramiding model of intellectual maturation. According to Piaget, a person's intellect develops through six stages of growth.[12] The drive to accomplish this climb of increasingly complex structures of thinking is genetic: we are born ready to develop intellect. But to make the climb successfully, one needs good health, exposure to many metaphors, tactile and sensory experiences, chances for challenge and discovery, and an ecology of emotion and spirit that is encouraging.

Metaphors gather and chunk lots of information or an unwieldy experience into a more manageable chunk of meaning.[13]
To say that I weigh two-hundred pounds is a symbolic representation of what it feels like to lift me. If you really want to know my weight, let me sit on your shoulders. I can represent that experience with the figures "200 lbs." I can use that representation or *analog* in conversation as a way of compressing the experience of my heaviness into a single expression. "200 lbs." crunches the experience of my mass into a manageable chunk.

In theology, I can speak of God as "Triune," or as a "Trinity." By so doing I have crunched my experiences of God as incarnation of Love in the

Table 7.2

CRUNCHED MEANING

WORDS

Church	Sin	Justice
Love	Christ	Hope
Salvation	Grace	Neighbor
Perfection	Trust	Friendship
Temple	Enlightenment	Wisdom
Spirit	Nothingness	Surrender
Yahweh	Allah	Nirvana

ART/OBJECTS/SYMBOLS

Cross	Egg	Ring
Star of David	Lamp	Manger
Chalice	Scroll	Bread
Baptismal Font	Scale	Altar
Candle Flame	Dove	Incense
Crescent Moon	Monkey	Prayer Wheel

LITURGIES/WORSHIP

Eucharist	Singing	Marriage
Baptism	Benediction	Consecration
Tenebrae	Pilgrimage	Watch Night
Confession	Vespers	Prayer Meeting
Funeral	Bar Mitzvah	Pilgrimage

GESTURES

Kneeling	Hugging	Joining Hands
Ashes on the Forehead	Kiss of Peace	with Others
Kissing the Torah	Crying	Beating Chest
Bowing	Folded Hands	Waving

MOVEMENT

Processions	Dancing	Bowing
Standing-Sitting-Standing	Clapping	Raised hands
Running	Jumping	Twirling

FESTIVALS

Sunday	Yom Kippur	Christmas
Sabbath	Purim	Ramadan
New Year	Easter	Pentecost
Ash Wednesday	Thanksgiving	Maundy Thursday

flesh, God as creator and judge, and God as spiritual presence into a single word. The word can then be used in liturgy, songs and discourse in a more manageable way than the description of the term.

In religious institutions we use all sorts of metaphors and analogies to collapse big ideas and large amounts of information into something "portable." They are crunched bits of meaning that can be experienced as metaphors without having to unpack them of all their implications. Yet at some time in a person's spiritual journey they *must* be unpacked and repacked personally like a sky diver taking responsibly for his or her own parachute. Consider the list of "crunched" meanings in Table 7.2. It is nowhere near complete. What meaning chunks are essential to you? Make your own list.

Metaphors are meaning building blocks that can stand in for full and "complete" knowledge until the fuller knowledge is discerned.
Here are two examples:

Freud's idea of an unconscious mind that does not speak but shapes our thoughts and actions was a provisional attempt at describing something true about personality and thinking. There was no Unconscious to observe, but the idea has served as a helpful metaphor for the elusive aspects of human mentality for the century or so since Freud. It served as "place keeper" until clearer analogies and descriptions were found. Today, Freud's metaphor may be thought of as standing for the many cognitive operations (especially the operations of the right cerebral cortex) we carry on while we concentrate on our conscious thoughts.[14]

Likewise, "light waves" was the way physicists described the propagation of light from source to eye. It served as a place keeper while better descriptions could be found for how light worked. Today, another more accurate metaphor has taken its place. Physicists now speak of packages of photons or "quanta" of light moving through space. This metaphor seems to be a more useful way of characterizing light.

The same thing happens in our faith thinking. Thanks to provisional faith metaphors, the people of the past have sent on their tentative understandings of God and the world. Let us not receive them so dogmatically that we fail to notice the "commas" implied in words like "Creator," "Lord," "Master of the Universe," or "Rock of Ages." That which is at the heart of things can only be *suggested* in our languages. Let us encourage each other to continue the work of imagining God and the world in metaphors but with commas instead of periods.

CHAPTER EIGHT

I Remember

MARSHALL MCLUHAN liked to say (as a critique of human nature) that we seem to steer into the future with only the help of a rear view mirror.[1] His observation was correct, but his commentary about the folly of that approach was off the mark. The only way we can navigate into the future is by using the stored past, by using our memories. The way we make sense of new things is by running the new experience past the models of the world we carry in our memory. All any of us really are is the composite of the memory and the style of behaving we have in storage.

This memory we have is not just a chronology of events and a repository of information. It is the totality of experiences, information, skills, meanings, and models we and our culture have designed together and have deposited in the neural pathways of the cortex.

Figure 8.1 summarizes the components of memory. There are, actually, three memory systems at work in our brains and nervous system: 1) a sensory registry or buffer that holds a sensation for a second or two, 2) a working memory or short-term memory of limited capacity that is our conscious awareness of thoughts and sensations, and 3) a long-term memory much like a storehouse of more or less permanent memories.[2]

How these three interact and inform our action, how different memories are stored in different ways and how experiences make it to long-term memory is the focus of this chapter.

WHAT IS MEMORY?

Memory can be defined at four levels: 1) cellular (individual cells participating with a set of cells that hold a memory), 2) neural pathways (a network of cells and axons that are linked chemically to activate a memory), 3) network configuration (one of several kinds of networks that hold different categories of memories), and 4) function (memory sets that are either information, skills, meanings, or goals). Thus if one were asked to define memory, the definitions would depend on how close you want to look.

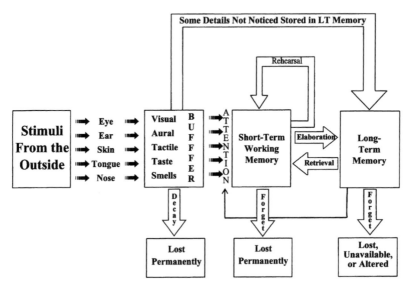

Figure 8.1
The Flow of Memory

Take as an example the memory you might have of your first dog. That memory (actually a cluster of memories) could be described from any of these levels:

- It can be described as what happened when a set of neurons and axons were electrochemically activated by input from the senses. The chemical changes and axon linkages created a memory of those inputs: your dog. The activated cells physically link with similar earlier memories making it possible to know what is going on. These dog memories are not located in individual cells, but on networks of cells spread out in many parts of the cortex. Individual cells, when stimulated by sensory experience, can activate the dog memory, but no single cell carries around "Fido." Rather, many individual cells have undergone physical changes to make the memory.
- It can be described as a complex pathway of cells and axons that are intricately linked to other neural pathways that, when stimulated by dog experiences, bring to mind YOUR DOG. These pathways are redundant and can withstand breaks and failures without losing the whole memory. Forgetting happens when the pathways are either unused for long periods of time, or suffer a breakdown in the way cells along the pathway "communicate" chemically with the others in the pathway.

- It can be described as a network of cells that is linked to other networks in a cross-referencing way that may (a) follow "rules" similar to grammar, (b) be linked by a cross-referencing of visual/spatial/physical characteristics, or (c) be linked by a cross-referencing of auditory characteristics. When your "dog memory" is activated, so is "dogness, "pet," "animal" and the like. When you see your dog, other doglike features are activated in your memory. When you hear your dog or remember its bark, other characteristics of the sound of dogs and dog-likeness are activated as well.
- It can be described in terms of the kind of memory it is, namely (a) information, (b) skills, (c) meanings, and (d) goals. So, with the help of your dog memory, you can have access to knowledge about dogs; ways to treat, care for and train pets; recognition of the value of dog and pets in your life and the role your dog plays in your life goals.

All four descriptions have in common the idea of linkages and pathways. That is the key to understanding how the brain holds memories. Imagine the human cortex as a jumble of thousands of roads, highways, intersections and paths all packed tightly into a very small landscape. Imagine an experience being like a vehicle entering the landscape through one of several gates. As soon as it enters the cortex landscape through one of these gates, its wheels pass over sensors in the pavement that send a signal to a traffic controller, allowing it to proceed or not. If it is allowed in, it is charged with energy (this is the role of the limbic system—to charge our experiences with feeling and focus our attention). If it isn't charged with energy, it stalls at the gate. If it gets energized, a specific pathway linking hundreds of these roads and intersections lights up creating a travel route. The cleared road ahead is a memory or set of memories. No sooner does the memory route light up, but hundreds of connecting roads light up as well (albeit not as brightly). Which of the alternate routes light up depends on the kind of "vehicle" that first entered the landscape, the nature of the main route and the clarity of road signs along the way. Routes that get traveled often get well defined and will be easier to travel, while the less used ones get overgrown, damaged and broken up to the point that they are useless.

Imagine that this highway system is a public works dream, because the more a route is used, the stronger, smoother, and more durable it gets. The more a route is linked to other associated routes, the more bridges and intersections it spontaneously erects. The more traffic it must accommodate, the more road signs it manufactures on its own. The best maintenance of the system is vigorous use.

Finally, imagine that like a real highway system, nearly every road and path is used by vehicles going to different places. A single intersection may participate in thousands of different and even unrelated routes. Some of the intersections and routes are used for both seeing (for example) and remembering the sight. The intersections and cell pathways can share in the recall of things as unrelated as the smell of cut grass and the state capital of Wyoming.

HOW DO WE GET A MEMORY?

Let's follow the steps to laying down a memory (refer to Figure 8.1) in this highway system. Specifically, let's see what happens when you learn the name of someone new to you so that you are able to recall the person and her name at another meeting. Let's say you have been introduced to a woman by a friend. Before any words register, the image of the person strikes the retina. The image of the person is held for a second or two in the visual buffer (probably in the retina itself) even as the image is sent on to the striate cortex. As long as you look at the person, the visual buffer is replenished and feeds the perception that is composed in the cortex.

Just how well you pay attention to these sensations is to a large degree dependent on the needs, meanings and agenda you carry with you all the time in your long-term memory and elsewhere. If the sensory buffers have things in them that are important to you, thanks to your midbrain you pay attention.

So, if your attention is turned to the woman, you hear her name as it is spoken to you. It is held in the auditory buffer and sent on the temporal lobes and other parts of the cortex to be interpreted as a female name. If you shake hands, the tactile buffer holds that sensation as it is also sent to the cortex. Some of the details of the sensory buffers, because they are important to you in unconscious ways, may be "filed" in long-term memory directly without your awareness.

The visual information, name, smells, touch and context of the meeting are held in your awareness in what is referred to as working or short-term memory.[3] This is your experience of what is going on. It is what you are aware of. It includes the sounds, images, smells and touch of the present moment PLUS the memories that are snagged and brought to awareness by the meeting. Those memories might include memories of other people this person reminds you of, ideas the person's name reminds you of, occasions her perfume makes you recall, and so forth.

Working memory is short-lived. If it is not refreshed, it will fade and much of it will be lost in seconds or minutes. Elements of the experience can be recalled to working memory if they have found a way into long-term memory, but the content of working memory is always shifting. There are, however, two ways experiences and thoughts can be kept "alive" in working memory: 1) by rehearsal (i.e., saying the person's name over and over again), and 2) by concentration (keeping one's senses on the object of attention).[4] The longer attention is focused on the experience, the more likely it will create a place in our cortex as long-term memory.

Not only is working memory volatile, it is limited in its capacity as well. There is disagreement among researchers as to how much we can keep in mind at one time. Some say seven facts, objects or numbers is the capacity of an average person's working memory. Others say that the capacity varies with the nature of what is being kept in mind. The current thinking now is that working memory manages three kinds of thoughts: 1) semantic and numeric thoughts (words, numbers, facts, or concepts) limited to the fewest items, 2) visual imagery (sights, spatial relationships, faces, pictures), the least limited, and 3) auditory experiences that are not words or numbers (sounds, music, noise, tone of voice, pitch), somewhere in between. Regardless of the kinds of things we keep in our awareness, working, memory is limited and easily forgotten without conscious effort.

Some of the aspects of an experience that may be important find their way into long-term memory without our efforts to memorize them. In the case of the woman in our hypothetical meeting, the sound of her voice, a gesture, or turn of a phrase might connect with some person or experience from your past in such a way that you will remember.

Normally, however, the person's name and other aspects of her presence will have to be rehearsed, studied and processed so that they get connected to some memory patterns you already have, as well as forming connections that are new. This is the process of elaboration.[5] Experiences, then, make the transition from working memory to long-term memory through a variety of cognitive elaborations. Here are six of them:

1. *Affective elaboration.* The strength of feeling attached to the experience helps determine its place and durability in long-term memory. When an experience and strong feeling are joined in memory the combination becomes a "word-event" (a combination of information and experience) and remembered as a single significant experience. The stronger the feeling, the more readily the memory is recalled (except in some cases of intense pain or trauma when our conscious selves inhibit the memory from becoming conscious).

2. *Rehearsal.* The time an experience or fact is kept vital in short-term memory helps determine its place in long-term memory. What we usually call rote memorization is this kind of elaboration.

3. *Repetition and practice.* The frequency of which a memory is recovered and practiced will help strengthen the memory. The process of becoming familiar with an experience or idea is this kind of elaboration.

4. *Reflection and connection.* The degree to which a memory is reflected upon, related to other memories, and integrated into a larger memory network, the more accessible will the memory be. A conscious decision to "dive" into the idea or experience to discover its depth of meaning will press it into long-term memory.

5. *Sharing meaning.* The more a person's memories are shared with other people, the better the chance of integrating the experience into a broader network of meaning (mating one's meaning with another's).

6. *Chunking.* The more our memories can be summarized and represented as symbols, phrases, analogues and rituals, the more durable they become as memories. As these meaning chunks are used, shared, affirmed, celebrated or applauded, the memory and meaning they represent are likewise celebrated and strengthened.[6]

The process is not finished once a memory pathway is etched. Each time it is recalled and mixed with other memories and new experience, the old pathway is changed. This is especially true of our biographical memories. Biographical memory consists of those self-conscious experiences of ourselves acting, thinking, and feeling. They make up the episodes that together comprise our personal narratives. John Kotre suggests that biographical memory is always being edited, augmented or out-and-out changed to maintain consistency, continuity and integrity.[7]

The six ways of elaborating information and experience drive working memory into long-term memory. Long-term memory, then, is the repository of facts, experiences, biography, stories, skills, meanings and goals held more or less permanently in the neural pathways of the cortex. They are constantly being shaped, shuffled, and organized by our innate hierarchy of physical, emotional, and metaphysical needs in concert with new experiences. Figure 8.2 summarizes these six elaborative strategies.

The way long-term memory is stored and retrieved is a function of the kind of memory it is. There seem to be several memory types to match the several senses and intelligences we all possess. For example:

1. For our ability to use and understand sentences, we have semantic memory.[8] This is the memory of things that are cross-referenced along word sounds and sentence structure categories (subject, verb, prepositions, adjectives, adverbs, and so forth).

2. For our ability to compose and understand our own biography and other stories, we have narrative memory.[9] Narrative memory is referenced to stereotypes, story parts, characters, scripts, dates, emotions and roles. These first two memory types start out as semantic memory in our short-term memory and then are stored differently in long-term memory.

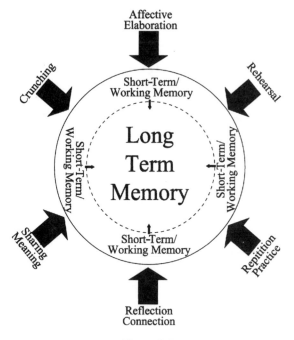

Like a pressure cooker, elaboration pushes our experiences into long-term memory.

Figure 8.2

3. For our ability to hear and comprehend noises (other than words), tones, music and sounds, we have auditory memory.[10] These memories are linked according to similarity of sound, events the sound is associated with, and the things the sounds come from.

4. For our ability to understand and create visual information (pictures, spaces, directions, proximity, faces, scenes, and the like), we have a corresponding way of organizing visual and spatial memories. These memories are linked by color, physical appearance, juxtaposition and the events such sights and spaces are the product of.[11]

5. For our ability to understand the things we touch, there is a corresponding way of storing and remembering tactile experiences. These memories are linked to similarity of texture, pressure, pleasure/pain and temperature as well as by the experiences that generate the sensations.

6. For our ability to understand taste/smell, there is a corresponding way of organizing and remembering taste/smell experiences. These memo-

ries are linked by similarity of taste, smell, texture and the experiences that generate these sensations.

Obviously, most things that become lasting memories are a combination of several (sometimes *all*) of these kinds of memory and experiences. There is hardly any experience we commit to memory that is strictly one kind or another. While our cortex knits these memory threads together with many patterns and cross weavings, it tends to gather the profusion of memory threads into several kinds of super knots. They include: EVENTS, CONCEPTS, RELATIONSHIPS, EMOTIONS and SKILLS.

You can test the cross-referencing power of these knots with some free association. On a large piece of paper put the name of a kind of event (such as BIRTHDAY). As fast as you can, around the paper write the names of as many birthday-related things you can think of. Draw circles around them and link them to others according to some obvious similarity. Continue to free associate in a similar way with each of the circles, drawing linking lines wherever they became clear to you. What you will have is a sort of hierarchical map of your birthday knot (refer back to Figure 2.2 in chapter 2 to see another knot clustered around "circus"). The hierarchy is reconstructed from specific experiences and memories, but the experiences combine into knots of generalities. This same thing is true of concepts and emotional states. There are others, no doubt, but these five memory knots are among the most powerful and dense.

Skill memories are different.[12] Instead of being thoughts that can be brought to consciousness, they are scripts that are executed rather than thought of. Certainly, a fact memory (like the definition of football) can bring to mind how to play the game, but the key to remembering a skill is a two-step process: remembering the experience within which the skill is required and starting to do the skill. Skill memory, such as place kicking a football, is not a set of hierarchical memories, but a linear set of "instructions." Some of the memory pathways are in the cortex, but some are in the nerve clusters along the spinal chord and other nerve trunks. They are even created with a different set of chemicals than are "fact" or "experience" memories.

Once the occasion for the skill is identified, the skill itself has to be initiated by the first step in the skill. Then, if it was learned well, the next steps follow one after another from start to finish. If you stop a place kicker in the middle of the routine, he or she may be able to tell you what the next step is but will have trouble telling you what the step after the step after the next is (much less how to do it). It has yet to be recalled. When it is, it may not be recalled into working memory but bypasses awareness altogether to instruct muscles, breathing, the senses, voice, and so on "orchestrated" by the cerebellum (see chapter one).

Long-term memory, then, is created when we are able to elaborate on new information and skills. These memories "exist" in either a mind-boggling network of pathways or sets of linear processes. How do they get recalled?

HOW DO WE RECALL?

Let's put memory in the context of another metaphor. Imagine our memories are like fish teeming in a well-stocked lake. Catching those memories and reeling them into consciousness is a matter of fishing and cutting bait. What I mean is that those memories don't leap into awareness by themselves. Rather, they have to be caught. They are caught by experiences, physical needs, and associations, by thinking and by other memories recalled. This lake has all sorts of fish in it. They may be as elusive as recollections, recognition, or familiar feelings. They can be as hefty as a fact, a story, or face. They may be rote memories like a poem, a song, or a speech, or reconstructed memories like the house of one's childhood or a friendship of long ago. They can be skills, postures, directions, shapes and sounds. These "schools" of memories are legion.

So how do we remember? Remembering happens when what is happening in working memory (awareness) or sensory buffers snags knowledge stored in long-term memory. Here are some of the baited hooks that snag memory:

WORDS READ AND HEARD	SOUNDS HEARD
QUESTIONS RAISED	MUSIC FELT
EXPERIENCES LIVED AND SHARED	OBJECTS TOUCHED
RELATIONSHIPS NURTURED	COMMANDS GIVEN
NATURAL SIGHTS SEEN	PROBLEMS ENCOUNTERED
ART EXPERIENCED	CELEBRATIONS RAISED
AROMAS SMELLED	A SKILL PERFORMED
TASTES SAVORED	PHYSICAL NEEDS FELT

You no doubt can think of more memory hooks that are effective at catching your memories. They are like hooks to our memories in that they cause a memory pathway to be activated and brought into the net of awareness. Each of us responds differently to these memory-catchers. Yet they all work to some extent, and when we do religious education it is important to cast with several hooks into each other's memory lakes. Figure 8.3 summarizes seven categories of memory "hooks." All seven are important to recall-

Educator's Tackle Box

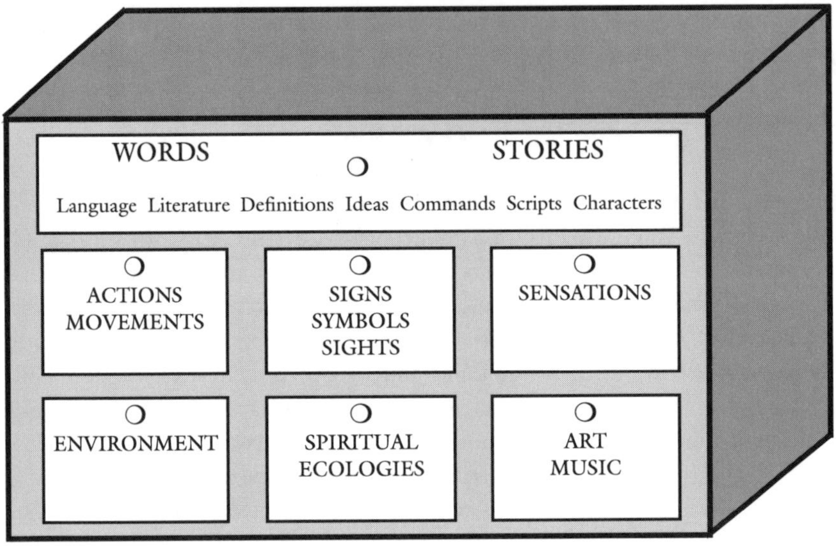

Figure 8.3

ing stored experience and knowledge. The educator's "tackle box" should include a variety of "hooks" and "flies" that can help people to remember. Consider these seven drawers of "hooks" and "lures":

- WORDS and STORIES:

This drawer is jammed. It includes words, definitions, commands, scripts, stereotypes, ideas and stories, events, literature, sentences and questions that bring personal memories to mind.[13]

- ACTIONS and MOVEMENTS:

Physically doing things will bring memories to mind. Performing a task or skill, assuming a posture, dancing, and so forth, can bring experiences into awareness.

- SIGNS, SYMBOLS and SIGHTS:

The things we see bring other things to mind. From drawings to photographs, from direction signs to icons, from faces to landscapes—all of these bring the stored past into the present.

- SENSATIONS:

Smells, tastes, sounds, textures, temperature, and the millions of combinations of these sensations bring worlds of memories to mind when learners are presented with them.

- ENVIRONMENTS:

Did you ever walk into a room and become flooded with recollections? Environments do that for and to us. They may be places you return to, simulations, natural ones or social ones. When learners are allowed to enter them, memories are tapped.

- SPIRITUAL ECOLOGIES:

Personal relationships and communities of people are special kinds of environment that deserve a drawer of their own. These are environments that evoke feelings, relatedness, values and roles that come from the strongest and deepest of our memories—our spirit. When we invite learners to take part in these ecologies of spiritual give and take, memories flood in. This drawer includes participation in dyads, small groups, large groups, play groups, worship groups, work groups, family groups, and whole communities.

- ART and MUSIC:

This drawer is an extension of the SENSATIONS and SIGNS, SYMBOLS, and SIGHTS drawers. Art and music are sensations with such strong spiritual and relational content that they ought to have a compartment by themselves to remind us of their value in helping people recall. The drawer includes paintings, sculpture, songs, instrumental music, and other arts.

In actual teaching, these lures and hooks are combined into complex experiences that take on a power of their own. Most of our educational plans include experiences that don't neatly fit into a drawer. I use the metaphor of the many ways we can access the memories of students.

WHAT IS FORGETTING?

You know the expression "Use it or lose it." This is true of memory—short-term and long-term. Forgetting is a matter of not elaborating a working memory so that no lasting pathways are formed in long-term memory. It is also a matter of not keeping a long-term memory active, thus destroying its cross-reference points with other memories. If I learn a person's name and use it for a day or two when she is around, that name is elaborated into long-term memory just by its repeated use. However, if I no longer have an occasion to use the memory and do not see or even think of the person for years, I may lose the memory. It may decay, or it may get isolated from a larger net. In either case, I have forgotten. Forgetting is the inability to bring a long-term memory into working memory. It happens when we fail to pay attention or elaborate, or it happens if we have one of several learning disorders that block accurate perception or elaboration.

The last hooks to memories that fade are those that have to do with sight and smell. I may have absolutely no recollection of a seventh-grade classmate, even when I am told my old friend's name, but I still may sense recognition if I am shown a picture. Or, a long-ago childhood experience may be inaccessible to me except for an aroma that brings it to mind.

TURNING RELIGIOUS MEMORIES INTO THE CONTENT AND FORM OF OUR BEING

One might define education as the process of getting meaningful memories. If memories form as experiences, and are elaborated and linked with what one already knows, then elaboration and remembering are central to education. Religious education is the process by which people make meaningful memories that serve to reconnect us with what is at the heart of things and with each other. The process is no different from any other kind of education: experience/linkage/elaboration. But it is intended to go a giant step further. It intends to assist in the transformation of one's manifesto, one's self.

To summarize:

- I began in the first two chapters by suggesting that we manufacture meanings and organize them into models of the world in the tissues of our brains. Against these models we compare new data and experiences making sense of things at ten levels of meaning. The outer six I have called our meta-physical meanings or manifesto. These meanings and models are held in our brain tissues.
- In chapter three, I proposed that the religious educator is one who is allowed to assist persons in the formation and transformation of the religious or "meta-physical" memories we live out of.
- In chapter four, the work of the educator was described more as memory and meaning midwife than as simply meaning delivery service. To be an educator is a humbling and deeply important task requiring an ethic built on human freedom and the sanctity of each person's world of meaning.
- In the fifth chapter, we looked at the way perception is influenced by memory and how the mechanism of perception can help us define the general approach to and content ("curriculum") of religious education. The "protocols of perception" provide leading questions that need to be asked about our meta-physical models of life.
- In chapter six I described how the rules of perception can guide educators in helping students build meaning. Special attention was given to the way the figure-ground protocol can help us in the creation of

environments of learning and worship. How a person is involved with a "meaning background" will contribute to that person's self-understanding.

- In chapter seven I gave special attention to an essential strategy for making meaning: metaphorical thinking. Humans are metaphor-makers. Metaphors are essential to our creation of language, central to creativity and the arts, and necessary to interpersonal communication. Likewise, faith-thinking and sharing depends on the use of and creation of metaphors.

- In this chapter (chapter eight), the mechanisms of making and recalling memories have been outlined, with emphasis on ways to apply them to religious education. At the heart of making meaning that is lasting is the ability to elaborate our experiences so they become part of our long-term memory network.

Some (if not most) memories people have are primarily tools and resources employed to live safely and successfully from day to day. Call these memories our stock of knowledge. It includes both information we can declare and skills we use for action.[14] Much of what secular education is aimed at is the increase of this stock. Religious education is aimed a bit differently. Certainly we are concerned with certain kinds of knowledge and skill, but fundamentally our aim is to assist people in the building of meaning by which they organize and direct their lives. These deeper meanings are built on and are much influenced by the stock of knowledge and skill, but has more to do with who a person is rather than what he or she knows. These memories I call manifestos and goals. They deserve to be chosen consciously by people. Religious educators help people choose who they are and help them to choose transformation. We do it by helping students to remember the meanings of the past and by helping them connect with the emerging meanings of the present.

TO SERVE, PROTECT AND LET BE

Whether what we recall are bodies of knowledge, skills, manifestos or life-directing goals, they are still memories. All of them get formed in about the same way, are stored according to similar rules and are recalled in similar processes. They are all things of mind and spirit that are held in brain cell pathways. Anything that affects those pathways—from propaganda to Prozac, from teaching techniques to television—is our concern. It is our concern because we are called to feed, nourish and transform each other by making memories. At the same time we are called to do it carefully, humbly safeguarding each other's freedom and integrity. Ours is not the work of the "memory police"; rather, it is the work of educators whose ethics are grounded in human freedom and propelled by faith in the plan our creator lavishly spread in the genomes of each person.

In the remaining four chapters I will offer a religious education strategy that puts elaboration, recall and transformation at the center of the approach and takes the principles of cognitive science to heart.

CHAPTER NINE

Driving Memory into Being

THERE IS A DIFFERENCE between knowing and being. I may know the "Golden Rule" or the "Shama" but that knowledge may or may not in-form my being, my self or my models of the world. Religious education seeks to in-form being with knowledge and experience so that the models of the world we live by are transformed. I offer these two stories on the relationship between knowledge, memory and being.

DANNY

Danny was four and a half when he began his summer at Pacific Oaks School in Pasadena, California. He was all smiles, even on the first day. He talked very little, but moved delightedly from one play area to another. He didn't play with other children at first, but he always seemed cheerful and ready to share his smile for selected split seconds. He was with the special group (made up of children with motor, perceptual, and verbal problems). Danny enjoyed running about but stumbled easily. He would take very large steps but would miscalculate his gait and trip. He was enough aware of his lack of coordination not to trust himself to climb. Running, crawling and riding were okay, but he would not leave the ground except in a swing.

During his second week at Pacific Oaks there was just too much activity in the trees and on the roof of the trike shed for anyone to stay on the ground. Danny asked one of the volunteers to help him onto the roof of the shed. He climbed cautiously and stood tall when he arrived at the top. He walked slowly across the thirty-foot length and back. He repeated his steps over and over. By the end of the day he was walking and stomping, with steps almost as long as he was, calling out to the others in the yard. Danny made it a habit to go to the shed roof every day after that to make his triumphant march back and forth. He was in control of his legs and his roof-world. Little Danny became Big Dan.

When a teacher asked how he was able to walk so well he said, "Well, see, my feet found out how to stomp and not stump." Each day he and the teacher would take a few minutes to talk about his experiences of walking, jumping and climbing and the teacher would suggest something new he might try. In the following weeks, Danny began to talk more and experiment with his climbing legs and stomping feet. As he developed his leg skills, his social ability changed for the better. The change was gradual, but it was obvious he was more comfortable around the other children and with his own body because of what he was learning. Danny had learned something deeply.

ROBYN

Robyn was sixteen. She was a member of the youth group at her church and was well loved by her peers. I was the counselor for the youth fellowship group. We had spent a few weeks thinking about and studying the reasons why some people are poor and some are not. In our Sunday morning classes, the young people shared some of the work of getting information about poverty. They discovered what the scriptures said about poverty and generosity. They scanned the newspapers for articles about life on the edge of and beyond economic ruin.

Robyn was only marginally interested in our study, but did her best to stay in tune with the class even though her life was focused elsewhere. I supposed she was typical of that group of middle class suburban teens in Southern California.

The end of the study (which came none too soon as far as the kids were concerned) included an overnight stay in a church in the heart of Los Angeles. We arranged to be there from right after school on Friday until Saturday evening. This was a time before gang activity had spread all over the inner city of Los Angeles, so most parents allowed their teen(s) to go. There were fourteen of us: two adults and twelve teens.

I must say that over the month of study about social problems and ethics, role playing and the Bible, the young people gained a lot of knowledge about the problem of poverty in our area . They had even made simple efforts to raise money and collect clothing for "the poor." They knew what Jesus had said about justice and poverty, about generosity and greed. They, including Robyn, were well informed for young suburbanites. Our "plunge" into the city tested our perceptions and knowledge.

On the afternoon of the second day, we had decided to spend some time in Pershing Square. It was a small park in the heart of the city where homeless, elderly, set-adrift people gathered for some community. There were people on all the benches—knots of people listening to soapbox orators, some playing chess or checkers, bag ladies and homeless men. Most were alone, many were in one sort of buzz or another, and most were old.

Robyn and three of her close friends had eased up to an old woman on a bench. She was heavy, overdressed, and had a couple of bags next to her. One leg was bandaged with paper and tape.

As soon as the four sat near her, she started to rant. She cursed and yelled for them to get off her bench, leave her alone and get lost. They were stunned.

I was standing off to the side of the park with an eye on the teens and was about to move in to extract them when they left. Robyn huddled with her friends. I could see she was upset and near tears. The four searched their pockets and came up with some money. They crossed the street to a drug-store and emerged five minutes later with two carnations on long stems.

They came back across the street to the grumpy old woman. Carefully, naively, Robyn and the three surrounded the woman. With words I can only guess at, they spoke to her. Robyn offered her the flowers.

When I asked her about the encounter, Robyn said the old woman was named Virginia. Robyn said the anger they first met from Virginia fell from her face like a loosened mask when they returned. They began to talk and Virginia told some of her story to these teenage intruders. She used to be a private secretary to a film producer; she retired but had no pension. With no family, she could only afford a flop house on Grand Avenue. She told them of getting sick and of being lonely as her seventy-fifth birthday drew near. They talked for about half an hour.

I have a photograph of the five of them: the kids pressed against Virginia and on the ground in front of her, talking to her and laughing. When I sig-naled that it was time to go, they all gave Virginia a hug. Virginia handed one carnation back to Robyn and patted her hand. As the kids walked away, Vir-ginia was crying.

We didn't talk about it for an hour or so. Back at the church Robyn prayed at supper. She prayed for Virginia and for us and for a way that she could change Virginia's world.

At the table we talked about our experiences. We recalled facts about our visit to Pershing Square that now had faces with them. Robyn remem-bered Jesus' words. She quoted them as best she could remember: "In as much as you have done it to the least of these, you have done it to me." The doctrine of the incarnation found a home in Robyn's being. Her model of old people, her model of the power of love, her model of her self, and her model of God were permanently altered. She already had big parts of this compassionate perspective alive in her. They were given to her by loving and generous parents. So Robyn wasn't going a new direction with her being; she was going deeper.

Both these stories point to the same thing: that what can be recalled or performed ultimately means very little until memories and skills shape one's being. Danny learned a skill. The Cerebellum finally got the right memory paths laid upon it to allow him to walk and balance, run and climb successfully. The deeper learning, however, was the transformation of the model he had of himself as he learned, reflected, and was affirmed in his new skill.

Robyn claimed a new concept. Meaning coalesced around ideas like

Figure 9.1

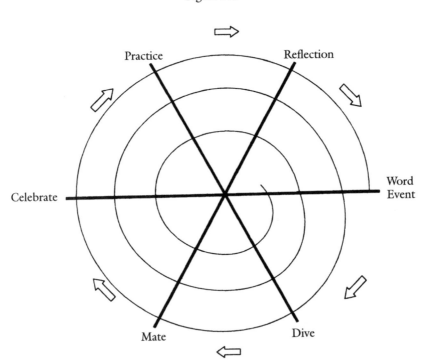

Effective learning takes a person through six elaborative processes. From one point of view the learning continually broadens one's models of the world. One gets a bigger picture as one learns. From another perspective, the spiral of learning deepens one's models of the world. That is, life-long learning makes a person more and more of an expert about what he or she has continued to learn. Both being an expert and getting a bigger picture of the world and our place in it is a function of these six elaborative processes that drive memory into Being.

generosity, kindness and acceptance. Attached to the ideas were memories of words and actions of a teacher two millennia back. The deep learning, however, was the transformation of the model she had of love's power, her self as a vessel of that love and of what was at the heart of human community.

Remember the definition of the religious educator from chapter three: **A religious educator is the one who delivers and draws out the memories, urges, information and experiences that serve to reconnect a person with what is at the heart of creation, with ultimacy.** To do religious education is to do those things that reconnect a student's life models—the student's very being—with the source of all that is. The result is transformation. My whole premise has been that the better we understand the way models are formed and transformed in the tissues of the brain, the better we can get on with the job of religious education. We cannot be satisfied with facts mastered, catechisms memorized, experiences stored and skills learned. We are after deeper learning than that of facts and skills. On the other hand, we cannot get to the meta-physical layers of human life unless we know how to teach facts, make memories and coach skills. We must do both.

THE TEACHING-LEARNING SPIRAL

The way from experience to meaning is a spiraling journey that continually passes six cognitive landmarks: 1) Word-event, 2) Dive, 3) Mate, 4) Celebrate, 5) Practice, and 6) Reflection. Walk with me around this teaching-learning coil (see Figure 9.1).

Word-Event

The first stop around the circle is an experience of a significant *word-event*. As was mentioned in the last chapter, a word-event is an experience wherein essential meaning is addressed in an affective way. Where information and feeling join, we learn.

What is essential meaning? In the chapter on perception, I outlined an array of questions that humans "ask" at the **intersection** of the six levels of **meta-physical meaning** and the **protocols of perception**. All human beings are confronted with the mystery of these questions. That is, we are always working at building and refining the models of Self, Community, Value, History, Future, and Cosmos. As the models become the center of our attention, one way or another, we ask: Why? What? When? How? Where? In What Context? When we encounter an emotionally powerful invitation to work at one of our essential models, we open up to answers, solutions and explanations to our search for meaning. When this kind of word-event happens, we will have taken the first important steps around the learning coil. In the story of Danny, the very environment of the school was a word-event. For Robyn, it was her encounter with Virginia.

Experiences, information, solutions and answers swirl around us all the time, but most go unnoticed or little remembered. However, when what is happening to us arouses feeling it is routed to the hippocampus to be tagged as important, "colored" by the feeling and sent to the cortex to lay down a memory pathway. The hippocampus is located deep within the brain where it is well protected and surrounded by the cortex. When the hippocampus is significantly damaged, new memories stop being made. Motor skills may still be learned, but the person with a certain kind of hippocampus defect will not remember having learned them. Without that tag, conscious experience does not make a lasting memory pathway in our cortex. The emotional tag does not have to be strong. It may just be a sense of arousal or heightened attentiveness, it may be the simple pleasure of discovery, but it must have some feeling quality to be remembered. The stronger the feeling, the deeper it is etched in memory. If this were not the case, we would be overloaded with memories in our first year of life. Even rote memory must be tagged as important or it will not last as a memory pathway.

In Danny's case, remembering walking-jumping-stomping skills had a lot riding on it. Leg skills were essential to his getting big, being autonomous and knowing who he was. In Robyn's case, she was only partially involved with the struggles of poor people and could have lost the memory of the causes of poverty or the meaning of incarnation had she not come to feel their value in her encounter with Virginia. Just in the nick of time, words and feeling found each other.

So when we educate, it is important to help a student's model-making intersect with his or her faith tradition so faith can inform models of the world. Not only that, the intersections need to be experienced in a way that arouses feeling and moves the student to pay attention.

Dive

The second stop around the circle is the *Dive*, patterned after Ross Snyder.[1] It refers to a student's private reflection on the personal meaning and value of a thing or idea. It is a solitary process. It includes brooding, thinking, creating, wondering, remembering, writing, painting, sculpting, and any other way of delving into the depths of meaning an event stirs up. To *dive* is to search a meaning to its depths, learn of its connection to other meanings, and to come up for air often enough not to get tangled in the jumble below.

Finally, the diver must get out of the pool, dry off and make an account of what he or she has discovered.

An educator needs to encourage the dive, instruct the diver, and offer ways for the student to report on the discoveries. Having aroused an interest and presented a word-event, we invite students to find the web of meaning and memory the word-event snagged. No one can do it for them. But every diver needs instruction and the knowledge that there is a companion on shore.

When Danny encountered the environment of Pacific Oaks School, at first he watched and brooded. Alone, he watched the other children climb. He came to terms with his ache to climb with them. With the encouragement of his teacher, he thought about it. She invited him to play out with dolls his desire to climb and jump. Danny put them on the tops of imaginary houses, making them jump and run and even fall. After a particularly painful fall before he ascended to the top of the toy shed, his teacher helped him up and asked, "How did it happen?" Danny tried to explain, but ended up reenacting his stumble. Even after the teacher left, Danny went over and over his accident. Then he sat. He was a master diver.

Robyn's dive began as a sort of wading at first, when we studied scripture and social conditions in a classroom. She didn't take a deep breath and submerge herself until the encounter with Virginia. Her whole afternoon following the visit with Virginia was spent thinking, wondering, and discovering ideas and feelings. She came up for air at the meal that night, ready to share the treasures the depths had given up.

Mate

The third stop around the circle is *Meaning Mating*. Call it dialogue, debriefing, discussion, sharing, show-and-tell or give-and-take. Whatever you call it, it is the experience of making known to another what the learner thinks and feels in a way that others can respond and mate experiences and meanings. The effect of mating is twofold: it gives the learners a chance to compose and organize word-events and dives, and offers an arena for building new meanings as ideas are combined and sharpened. The educator can facilitate mating by convening groups who have shared an experience, are working on similar meanings, or have an interest in similar skills. The educator needs to be ready with leading questions or assignments that will bring the minds of the pair or group into some sort of confluence.

How an educator encourages learners to share ought to reflect the many "intelligences" we have. We need to be ready to facilitate mating that runs the gamut of the arts and engages all the senses. Talking, drawing, singing, acting, dancing, building, and all their combinations, can give learners means of sharing meaning. In the process of mixing up meanings, ideas start to emerge.

Celebrate

The rudimentary meaning of *celebrate* is: to take from hiding for all to see and understand. At the Mass, a priest celebrates Christ's presence in the Eucharist by lifting the host for the congregation to see. The host carries and reveals the meanings of Eucharist, gospel, grace and the Christ in a tangible moment.

Most of our essential meanings get assembled in metaphors and symbols. A nation's flag is a symbol of its ideals; the Torah is a symbol of the Presence and Law of Yahweh; a monument symbolizes the courage and valor of fallen soldiers. We invent such carriers of meaning all the time, personally and as a community. We gather a cluster of meanings and put them into a word, song, work of art, dance, or story that evoke the meanings. The meanings reside in a symbol (they have been crunched). Then, if the symbol can be lifted and affirmed for others to recognize, celebration occurs. Celebration further presses meaning into one's being. It is also a way that meanings and models become part of the shared culture of all who participate in the celebration.

Danny learned, reflected, and even mated his learnings about who he was and how he could walk. As his new self became familiar, he developed a celebration every time he came to school that summer. He would make it his practice to greet the morning by climbing to the top of the shed, walking to the edge, stomping his foot and yelling, "Hey!" It was his celebration in a dance that hosted the person he had become, and it was for all to see.

After Robyn prayed at the evening meal, she got up and left as the rest of us began to eat. She returned with the carnation Virginia had given back to her. She had placed it in a drinking glass and put it in the midst of us. It was host to the meanings of the day and helped us to celebrate kindness silently, listening and the power of gentleness. What we, and Robyn in particular, had learned was transforming our models of the social world and God's place in it.

Practice

Søren Kierkegaard wrote once about the difference between being an admirer and a follower as he reflected on being Christian. He simply said that being awed and impressed by Jesus is not what makes one a disciple.[2] One must go beyond admiration of the master and be different, act different, follow the one admired. He was speaking as a Christian but his observation can be applied to anyone who has admiration for a leader, an institution or an ideal. It is possible to affirm a model of the world, celebrate it and extol its value and yet not let it transform one's actions. In the final analysis, people do not get transformed unless their reformed models result in transformed behavior.

So the next point around the learning coil is *Practice*. If an educational process avoids practice, the meanings may never get pressed into a student's being. The final elaborative step is to act as though you are what you celebrate. A would-be swimmer can study and understand the mechanics of swimming forever, but until that person swims again and again, he or she will not be a swimmer. I may study and understand justice, but until I do what is just, defend justice, oppose injustice, I am not a righteous person. Education must burst out of the classroom, sanctuary or home and into the streets to allow learners to become what they celebrate and affirm.

Reflection

I characterized the learning cycle as something like a spiral. Each time a learner goes around the coil, the process seems to start over again. Every practice can become a new word-event requiring fresh reflection and diving to discovery. It helps if the learner is a part of a learning community that helps each member continue along the journey of growth. The rhythm of learning can best be sustained in such a community of reflection and support. Some call the process "praxis."[3] I call it learning and it is the way models of the world take shape in the brains of humans.

This spiral can serve as a way of conceiving how experience makes its way into model building. In addition, it can serve as an outline for planning learning experiences. Figure 9.2 is an example of the spiral applied to a lesson. Try applying the spiral to your own lesson.

I have included a sample list of teaching/learning strategies that can be applied to the six stages of model building. These strategies, when employed in a curriculum agenda and learning goal, can fashion an effective learning event. Figure 9.2 is a sample lesson plan based on the spiral. It will serve as an example of the applicability of the ways experiences can be elaborated into one's models of life.

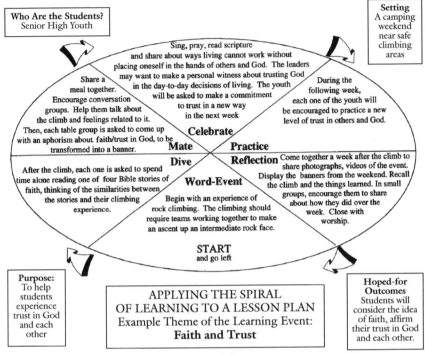

Figure 9.2

A LAUNDRY LIST OF STRATEGIES
(Also see the Tackle Box in chapter eight)

1. **Word-event** (alone or in a group)

drama	dress up	film/video
story teller	game	simulation
museum visit	concert	demonstration
field trip	panel	debate
puppet play	filmstrip	expert testimony
flannel board	CD Rom	ballet
musical	overhead	worship
projection	sermon	sacrament

2. **Dive** (alone)

write a poem	keep a journal	draw/diagram, sculpt
sing	pray	read, think/brood
research	observe	listen to music
sleep	play	meditate

take a walk / paint / compose
doodle / take photographs / make a videotape
make lists / climb a tree / think of metaphors
pretend / brainstorm

3. Mate (in pairs, groups)

talk / plan a menu / do group discussion
show/tell / give/take / play a game
role-play / compose / sculpt
make pottery / build / ask questions
summarize / create symbols / read aloud
fish bowl / fix a meal / plan a party
study Bible / share photos / make a film
evaluate

4. Celebrate (in pairs, groups)

worship / share a meal / dance
play / sing / take part in a procession
praise/pray / work / attend a funeral
go to a wedding / watch a sunrise / see a movie
shout / whisper / look at the sky
keep silent / take a walk / do sports
recite a poem / do a litany

5. Practice (one or two, or in groups)

do fund-raising / feed the hungry / do a service project (like Habitat for Humanity)

write a legislator / pray / work on changing lifestyle

lead a worship / give a talk / try being more observant
teach a class / be a liturgist / sing in a choir
present a play / present a musical / clean up a beach
be a tutor / visit the sick / care for an elderly person
make a new friend / write letters

6. Reflection (in groups or alone)

discuss / share feelings / do research
evaluate / role-play / make metaphors
affirm / list insights / watch practice video
summarize / talk about what's happened / pray

keep a journal / seek out experts
put learnings into painting, song, poem, sculpture, dance, symbols, etc.

CHAPTER TEN

*The Sevenfold Path
to Religious Intelligence*

MUSIC MAN

GARY IS A MUSIC MAKER. He carries a harmonica with him wherever he goes, ready to join a hymn at church or a ballad on the radio. He can play back a piece of music on the piano after one hearing. He plays keyboard in a band, he has been recorded on a couple of albums, and his friends say he has perfect pitch. On occasion he has tuned a guitar, autoharp or violin perfectly without a reference pitch.

Gary is suffers from severe mental retardation. He was institutionalized as a child and now (at about age forty) must be supervised. Still, Gary makes music with the best of them. If we were a race of music makers, he would be considered a genius.

For most of human history Gary, and those like him, have been stigmatized as stupid, dumb or slow, without regard to that part of their intellect wherein they excel. They expose the chauvinistic way we evaluate a person's intellect. I do not want to minimize the serious cognitive impairment Gary and people like him must endure, but seldom is the impairment duplicated in all segments of their intelligence.

The very idea that a single IQ test could quantify a person's mental ability is being scrutinized anew by educators. The overwhelming evidence is that intelligence is not *one* thing but has several components. The belief that a standard test could quantify the intellectual skill of all people of all cultures, races, and sexes, is no longer held by cognitive scientists and educators, and as soon as educational politics gets out of the way, perhaps then the facts can inform public and higher education.

True, Gary cannot handle complex logic, interpersonal nuances, or linguistic subtleties the way most people can, but his intellectual deficiency is not global. He is my reminder that human brain power is multifaceted and that we have too long treated intelligence as unitary. He reminds me also that each ability requires different ways of teaching, training and nurturing.

The tragedy is not just that Gary, and those like him, are ignored and their other gifts left untrained. The greater tragedy is that public and private education for "normal" children is usually aimed at only one or two modes of thinking. In typical ways of thinking about making people "intelligent," only the exceptionally gifted ones in other than math and language get the training they need.

While a great deal of public education is stuck in the verbal-mathematical-logical ghetto, the entertainment industry and some businesses have found new territory in which to pioneer. These are the spatial, musical and visual frontiers of cable television, desktop video production, electronic games, computer "multimedia," and the internet. They are shaping human abilities that traditional education tends to leave alone. In fact, they are shaping the world models of young people today simply by using methods that go beyond the printed word. These developments demand fundamental change in our approaches to education. At the very least, the "information revolution" is pointing to the next directions for education: self-directed learning, random access to information, integration of many subjects to tackle single problems, visual-spatial information processing, and learning several things at the same time.

Actually, these directions are not new. Perhaps they seem new to formal education of this past half century, but people have always learned best at their own initiative and rate by getting bits of information in a random way and by using their whole brains. It wasn't Microsoft who brought to humanity the grammar of icons and pictures—the neanderthal icons of the Lascaux caves in France or the hieroglyphs of Egypt remind us of the way pictures and words have always been a part of human communication.

FAITH IS MORE THAN WORDS

What has this to do with religious education? In churches and synagogues the dominant approach to religious thinking is linguistic and logical. To be religious from this perspective is to be able to speak, pray, reason with, listen to, read, and hear *words*. These words, if they are powerful and right, ought to lead to religious action and experience. Music, the arts, movement, quiet introspection, and interpersonal relationships, however, are only side dishes for the main course, which is a huge helping of *words*. A quick look at curriculum materials published by various religious publishing houses will confirm the place of verbal-logical reasoning in being steadfast in faith and learning about faith. I am not referring to the fact that the materials are printed (although that is a reflection of the limitation of this verbal-logical perspective); rather, I refer to the stated purposes a curriculum writer offers to a teacher and student. The course outcomes usually aim at a linguistic result: students will be able to write, tell, say, explain or read something of their faith. With language being so central to our lives, it ought to occupy an important place in religious education, but not to the exclusion of other intelligences. Seldom does a writer of curriculum expect the students to:

sculpt	control their heart rate
commune with nature	listen to an environment
fast	cook
hammer a nail	meditate
dig a ditch	give back massages
change a diaper	draw
daydream	dance
make films	sing
visit a shut-in	play an instrument

as religious ends in themselves. If those sorts of activities are included in the lesson suggestions at all, they are teaching tools or methods, not religious education objectives.

Human beings are speaking, reasoning creatures and so logic put into words is central to the way we make sense of our experiences, express our manifestos and excel cognitively. However, we are more than just speaking, reasoning mammals. There are other kinds of excellence that make up human intellect. There are other modes of being that lead us to reunion with what is at the heart of things.

SEVEN INTELLIGENCES

Thanks to the work of Howard Gardner and a team of researchers at the Harvard Graduate School of Education, we have a new way of imagining intelligence. Gardner's research conclusions were first described in *Frames of Mind*, published in 1983.[1] Here is some of what he and others have discovered:

- We can excel in at least seven ways of thinking: linguistic, logical-mathematic, musical, kinesthetic, spatial, interpersonal, and intrapersonal.
- These seven ways represent seven different intelligences in human cognition. Everyone has these cognitive abilities in varying strengths.
- Very few people are excellent at every one of them. All seven, however, represent the range of thought processes, information and skills that roughly define the human repertoire.

- In other words, the seven intelligences describe the range of human excellence. They help define us.

For Gardner, a cognitive ability has to meet four criteria in order for it to be classified as an intelligence.[2] Consider these four criteria.

1. An intelligence can be quantified so that one person's ability can be compared with another's.

2. An intelligence originates from a particular part or parts of the brain. Some skills may use more of the right cortex (like musical and spatial intelligence), and others will utilize more of the left cortex (like linguistic and logical-mathematical). Likewise, some skills will use more of the left and right occipital lobes (like spatial intelligence) in the rear of the brain, some will use the center of the cortex (like body kinesthetic intelligence), and others will use more of the left and right frontal lobes (like interpersonal intelligence). If the ability can be found to have discrete places in the brain for most of its operations, it meets this criteria.

3. The potency of one intelligence is independent of the potency of other intelligences. That is, one ability's strength does not predict the strength of another.

4. An intelligence is used for problem solving.

All seven abilities meet the criteria for an intelligence. Now, we will look at each one.

Linguistic Intelligence[3]

The ability to speak, understand, read, and use language creatively must be at the apex of the seven abilities. Language allows us to pull experiences together so they can be passed on. There are other forms of communication, but none so adaptable and accommodating as the flow of words. This intelligence has to do with knowing and creating verbal patterns. The skills involved include (but are not exclusive to):

talking	reading
writing	sign language
language acquisition	story telling
comprehending words	

In religious life, this intelligence serves us as we read scripture, talk and write of our religious pilgrimages, learn to read ancient languages, do research, create poetry and prayers, and listen to the words of others. Some of those who excel in this intelligence are preachers, story tellers, writers, poets, and scholars. They combine other of their intellectual gifts through the excellence of their linguistic ability.

Spatial Intelligence[4]

We live in three physical dimensions. Making our way from place to place, remembering the way to get from one spot to another, and knowing where one is in a larger context makes it possible to navigate in the physical world. Spatial intelligence has to do with seeing and knowing spatial patterns, shades, colors and connections. It has to do with our artistic abilities expressed in pictures and shapes. This intelligence manifests itself in one's ability to:

remember a route and follow it	read a map
make a map	know where something is
know compass points	understand and identify shapes
solve visual puzzles	sculpt, draw, paint, build
use and invent visual spatial metaphors	imagine visual images
imagine the relative positions of things	recognize faces

This intelligence serves us as we understand maps; find our way in a building, city or landscape; and remember where things are. It makes it possible for us to express meanings, faith, events and stories in the graphic arts. Painters, sculptors, and other artists that use visual media have played an important part in the creation and transmission of religious culture. In addition, every member of a faith community worships and learns in an environment surrounded with visual expressions. Spatial intelligence is essential to human culture. Thus it is essential to human religious culture as well.

Musical Intelligence[5]

Pitch and rhythm have meaning to us. To one degree or another all of us make use of them to express ourselves. To be excellent in our ability to organize them into meaningful patterns is to make and/or understand music. This intelligence includes these abilities:

singing	playing a musical instrument
composing music	writing music
enjoying music	understanding music
voice inflection	praise and celebration

We call on our musical intelligence when we sing songs about our faith, use musical instruments to set a mood, or transform an environment. We use this intelligence in our praise and worship, seasonal celebrations and even personal devotions. Our cantors, choirmasters, and song leaders use their musical excellence to help the faith community declare its faith and spirit.

Figure 10.1

INTELLIGENCE IS NOT ONE THING BUT SEVERAL

Intelligence is defined as a mental ability over which we have conscious command and satisfies these four criteria: 1) The ability is an essential intelligenee that enables us to solve problems, model the world and is a means of expression. 2) The ability is governed by specific parts of the brain. 3) The ability can be measured. 4) The ability exists independent of the other intelligences.

Logical-Mathematical Intelligence[6]

The ability to know and figure out patterns of cause and effect, and to make calculations, reflects our logical mathematical intelligence. This intelligence allows us to project futures and discern patterns of the past. It includes these abilities:

deductive logic	inductive logic
arithmetic logic	prediction
scientific method	calculation of amounts
taking measure	estimating amounts

Faith seeks understanding. Making sense of our affirmations requires the skills of logic, integration and inquiry. When we do theology, philosophy, and the pursuit of our curiosities, we are using this intelligence.

Body Kinesthetic Intelligence[7]

The ability to understand and perform meaningful and functional movements with one's body is our body kinesthetic intelligence. To know and perform these movement patterns is to express this intelligence. It includes these abilities:

walk	dance
run	jump
fall	do mime
gesture	climb
crawl	balance

We use our kinesthetic abilities in the faith community when we participate in ceremonies and liturgies that require gestures and postures. We use them when faith is expressed in dance or movement. It is involved in dramatic recreations of our faith stories, and in the gestures we use when we greet, nurture and converse with each other.

Interpersonal Intelligence[8]

We humans also have an intelligence about the way we relate one-to-one and in groups. This intelligence refers to a person's ability to know and create patterns of emotion, spirit and power between himself or herself and others. It includes:

awareness of differences between people	leadership
empathy with others	sympathy for others
understanding body language	understanding voice inflection
identification with others	sensitivity to others' emotions

It takes a special kind of intelligence to live in community and covenant with others. At its core is an awareness of the commonalities and uniquenesses that exist among people who live in *troth*. It shows itself as friendship, love, respect, understanding and sensitivity. It is necessary for social and ethical living.

Intrapersonal Intelligence[9]

Finally, we have an intelligence about what is going on in our own psyche and spirit and how to nurture ourselves. Self-awareness and consciousness is

Figure 10.2

WHAT INTELLIGENCE MAKES POSSIBLE

	The Ability to Model Our Worlds Using . . .	The Ability to Find Solutions . . .	The Ability to Express Meaning in Action by . . .
Musical Intelligence	Musical Models of Our Physical and Metaphysical Worlds	To Problems of Feeling, Community Community and Meaning through Music	Singing Composing Playing Instruments
Kinesthetic Intelligence	Models of Our Physical Body and its Place in a Space	To Problems of Work, Play, Sport, and Community through Movement	Dancing Gesturing Playing- Working
Interpersonal Intelligence	Models of the World of Our Social and Spiritual Ecologies	To Problems of Relationships and Social Life through Interaction	Loving Caring Cooperating
Intrapersonal Intelligence	Models of Ourselves Past, Present and Future	To Problems of Identity and Self-Understanding through Reflection	Self-Love Self-Care Self-Evaluation
Logical- Mathematical Intelligence	Logical and Numerical Models of Our Physical and Metaphysical World	To Problems of "What," "Why," "When," and "How Much" through Math and Logic	Calculating Reasoning Explaining
Spatial Intelligence	Spatial Models of Our Physical and Metaphysical Worlds	To Problems of "Where," "How," "When," "What" and "Why" by the Use of Spatial Thinking	Graphic Artistic Expression Making- Fashioning
Intelligence Linguistic	Linguistic Models of Our Physical and Metaphysical Worlds	To Problems of Communication through the Use of Words	Speaking Reading Writing

at the center of this intelligence. It has to do with understanding and creating patterns of feeling, and also with meaning which concerns one's own inner life, one's identity. It includes:

self-awareness	consciousness of feelings
consciousness of health	consciousness of needs and aspirations
meditation	reflection
goal-setting	prayer
self-evaluation	self-esteem

Personal spiritual life goes in two directions at once: Outward toward community life and inward toward an inner life. How well the journey *in* is traveled depends on one's grasp of one's own inner world of feeling and meaning. Traditionally, this intelligence helps us pray, meditate, confess, experience gratitude and need, dread and joy. If one of the results of a religious journey is being transformed (we use words like "born again," "saved," "redeemed," "found," "welcomed home," "enlightened"— depending on our tradition), then this intelligence too is central to our religious life.

Figures 10.1 and 10.2 spread out these seven intelligences with notes about how they are manifested (10.1) and about how they make meaning-making possible (10.2).

It is through these excellences, these abilities, that we model the world, solve problems and express ourselves. It is because of these cognitive processes that we can engage the world and make ourselves known within it. We have the task of passing on a religious culture by using these excellences as means of educating. We have a responsibility to train meaning-makers to use all seven of their abilities to INVENT culture as well. Thus, we need to be about the task of appealing to and developing ALL these intelligences and encouraging the application of them to religious life.

DR. DALE'S CONE REVISITED

For several decades lay and professional educators have used a simple diagram devised by Dr. Edgar Dale, professor of education at Ohio State University, that shows the relationship between teaching methods and retention. Figure 10.3 represents his idea. It has been used to remind teachers how important it is to present lessons that involve the whole person and all the senses in ways that are as much like real experience as possible. Some have taken the thesis to mean that the use of words and linguistic intelligence is inferior to other methods and intelligence. I want to propose that there *is* a

Figure 10.3

Dale's Cone of
Educational
Effectiveness

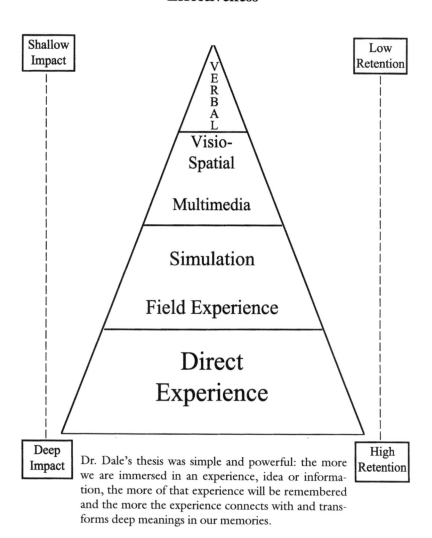

Dr. Dale's thesis was simple and powerful: the more we are immersed in an experience, idea or information, the more of that experience will be remembered and the more the experience connects with and transforms deep meanings in our memories.

Figure 10.4

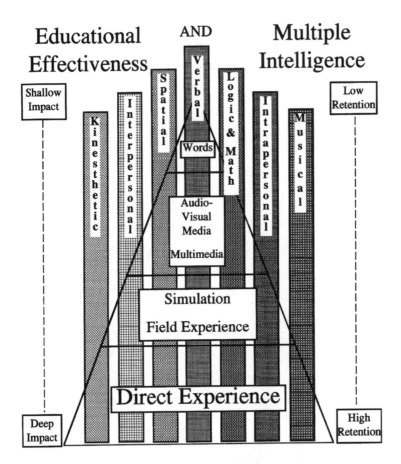

Dale's insight highlights the way direct experience tends to involve all or most of the intelligences of a learner. The further "up" the cone, the fewer abilities are tapped and the less impact the method has on the learner.

relation between teaching methods and retention but that it isn't a relationship that identifies one intelligence as superior over others. Rather, the relation has to do with the number of the intelligences that are called upon to claim and assimilate an experience. Of course, the content of what is being taught is more important than methods of teaching, but method is a close second. Dale reminds us of the importance of involving the whole self in the learning experience, and how much more involving doing is than seeing or hearing. The theory of multiple intelligence shows us what it means to "involve the whole person" in an experience. Figure 10.4 combines Dale's ideas with multiple intelligence theory.

WHAT ABOUT RIGHT AND LEFT BRAIN THINKING?

In the early fifties, neurosurgeons developed a surgical procedure for relieving the symptoms of some types of epilepsy. The procedure opened the door to three decades of research and speculation about the "bilateral" nature of the cortex. The surgeons cut the connecting nerve bundle between the left and right cerebral cortex of an epileptic's brain. It stopped the seizures in many epileptic sufferers.

Researchers such as Nobel-prize-winner Roger Sperry noticed subtle changes in the behavior and thinking of the patients who underwent the surgery. The patients seemed to have two brains in one skull. Their discoveries appeared to show that the two hemispheres could think almost independently, could even have conflicting thoughts, and could initiate conflicting behaviors. By cutting the corpus callosum that allows information to spread directly from one side of the cortex to the other, they were able to stop the seizures that incapacitated victims of epilepsy. In the process they observed how the two sides seemed to process information and accomplish behaviors in different ways.[10] Their work and research that followed gave rise to the popular idea that the human brain is actually two brains connected by nerve tissue that lets the two halves exchange information, and that the way one side thinks is different from the other.[11]

In chapters one and two some of the conclusions that "split brain" research has generated were described: how the right brain tends to be the side that processes information globally, and intuitively, and makes sense of visual, and spatial information; how the left side processes information sequentially and logically, and makes sense of words and numbers.[12]

The implications for education were immediately obvious: Schooling ought to educate the whole person by nurturing and feeding both sides [of the brain] in ways that are both verbal-logical, and visio-spatial. In a culture that puts so much emphasis on words, talk, calculation and logic, split brain theory is a welcome reminder that reading, writing, and math do not add up to the total scope of a person's education.[13]

In the meantime, the discoveries of other specializations in the cortex have given rise to a more detailed map of the cortex and its many abilities, most of which draw on the capacities of both hemispheres of the cortex. Indeed, some (like sight) draw on the back of both hemispheres while others (like planning and goal setting) draw on the right and left frontal lobes of the cortex.

Does this disturb the simplicity of "split brain" models of cognition? Perhaps only slightly. "Split brain" theory is like a two-dimensional description of a three-dimensional object. There are two styles of thinking and organizing experiences. But if we are to pursue religious excellence, it will be done by helping students develop the religious power of all seven types of intelligences. If we are going to be nurturing, rearing, teaching, training, informing, and equipping people in their religious quest, then the seven intelligences describe the seven parts of intellectual excellence we will need to feed.

Meanwhile, much continues to be written about the right and left hemispheres of the cortex and how different cognitive abilities and thinking styles are generated from one side or the other. The discoveries have opened up new areas of research and understandings about styles of thinking and the appropriateness of educational methods. The conclusions about whether people are right- or left-brained, however, have not proved to be particularly productive. The more productive approach to this discovery of "lateralization" has been to focus on the differences and uniquenesses of our various cognitive functions regardless of their location in the brain. There really isn't a right- or left-brained personality. We are more complex than that. The "split brain" theorists were right to criticize the unitary approach to human cognitive ability, but they stopped too short by proclaiming that we think bilaterally. We think, create and calculate in multiple ways. Since our intelligence is multiple, we ought to train and nurture these intelligences in multiple ways.

Over a person's lifetime of learning and learning to think, these thinking abilities grow and shift in importance. In the next chapter we will look at the ways human growth and development are affected by and affect cognition.

CHAPTER ELEVEN

Pilgrim Mind

CLEARING

ON A LATE SUNDAY AFTERNOON sometime during my thirteenth year, I happened to be sitting in the back row at a youth meeting at my church. It was not a remarkable gathering, just one like many others. I don't remember what was being talked about or why we were gathered, but I remember a vivid moment of self-awareness. The speaker droned on as I sat in a teenage haze. Then, a glare of sunlight from the leg of the metal chair in front of me caught my attention and my haze lifted in a perfectly clear epiphany: I knew myself; I had a feeling of "me." I thought something like this:

> *I* am sitting here. *I am* seeing this glint of light. It strikes my eyes in a way that is unique to *me*. Whatever the next moment brings, at *this* moment I am awake, alive and in possession of myself. I am not trying to be anything to anybody. I am not worried about anything. I am alive here and now as much as I can be. I think I will claim this moment as my awakening. Even as its importance begins to fade with that glare, I promise myself never to forget this moment.

The moment faded but I was left with a vigor that lasted for the rest of the day. It was as though I had been wandering in a fog when suddenly my head punched through to clear air and the clarity jolted me awake. The insight came and went inside of a couple of minutes, and nobody in the room knew of the little side trip I had been on. It wasn't the sort of glamorous or glorious "a-ha" moment of the stereotyped religious experience, but it was and still is a marker in my own journey of meaning. In a few minutes I had slumped back into the fog, only slightly aware of who I was and what I had experienced.

In that brief moment I stepped into a clearing along my life journey. In that clearing I knew a new depth of self-awareness and consciousness. I knew I was the same boy I was the day before, but I had gotten hold of something new. *I* was new. I was aware of myself as both a changeling and as an

integrity. I knew that my life would be a succession of clearings and transformations, but the one who moved through those changes would remain
me.

THE BRAIN AS CUPBOARD AND CAULDRON

The incident came back to me as I contemplated this chapter on human
development and spiritual growth. My thesis is that the human brain is the
physical nexus that holds our personhood. Our brains are physically designed
to make us cognitive and spiritual changelings headed toward wider and
deeper awareness of ourselves, of others, and of our physical and social ecologies and our worlds of meaning. The way the brain is organized, the way the
tissues communicate, the thousands of innate programs we are born with
and the way accumulated meaning weaves us into the ecologies of human
community—all this convinces me that human beings are *naturally* spiritual
pilgrims. What's more, the *focus* of our spirituality is an ever-changing one as
meanings build on meanings over a lifetime. My conviction is that this lifelong accumulation of meaning, this pilgrimage of mind and spirit is rooted in
chromosomes, chemistry and tissues, but transcends our biology. Human life
is at least a brain on a quest, a mind in pilgrimage.

Religious educators are called to assist in the spiritual pilgrimages of
those who would allow us to be their teachers and companions along their
way. We need to pay attention to the insights of neuroscience, letting them
shape our vision of unfolding human nature.

Cognitive science and neuroscience teach us that a person's brain is
both a sort of cupboard and a cauldron. It is the physical container of meanings, memories and manifesto (i.e., one's spirit), and at the same time it is
that which cooks, combines and stirs the contents to make of human experiences what they become. To put it another way, the central nervous system is
both the birthplace and nursery of our developing souls. This soul called
Jerry Larsen wasn't deposited in my brain at birth; it was conceived, born
and nurtured by the mating of my biology and my social ecology. This chapter will look at the implications of this developmental view.

SPIRIT

I need to back up. Just what do I mean by the words *spirit* and *spiritual*? The
literal meaning of the Latin word *spiritus* is "breath." In the Hebrew, the
word that gets translated as spirit stands for life given by God to each living
thing. From those root words, the concept has grown and accumulated vol-

umes of meaning. At the very least, human spirit refers to our inner life and its quality.

One's spirit can be said to be good or evil, so spirit has **an ethical dimension**. It can be said to be the essence of a person, so it has to do with **identity and one's manifesto**. One's spirit can be said to **transcend physical limits,** so we think of it as metaphysical. One's spirit can be described as high or low, so a person's spirit has degrees of **vitality.** We talk of sharing our spirit or withholding it, so it is bound to human **relationships and group life**. Spirit is the essential aspect of human nature that gets "turned on" at birth and finds its color and intensity in the pilgrimage of one's life cycle. The opposite of spirit is lifelessness.

SPIRIT is our God-given life force that has these five potentials (see Figure 11.1):

Vitality: a degree of physical, intellectual, and emotional liveliness

Morality: a degree of fidelity to principles

Generosity: a degree of investment of one's self in and sharing with others

Identity: a sense of who one is in total, including a conviction about one's vitality, morality, and generosity

Consciousness: a self-awareness within the context of the important worlds of meaning within which one moves.

Each of these qualities are potentialities held in our brain tissue. One's spirit is born of flesh and blood.

To express it personally, my spirit is me. I am the embodiment of some kind of spirit. It is myself, my identity, my vitality, my values, my culture, and what I stand for. It's the sum of my hopes, my hurts, my hangups. Those hopes, hurts and hangups address each day with a particular style and combination of trust and dread, of enthusiasm and lethargy, of openness and clenchedness. That's my spirit.

When I say my spirit is low or high or anxious or calm, I am saying that I am feeling low or high or anxious or calm. I am spirit.

One's spirit *journey* is the history of seeking, missing and attaining these spiritual qualities, of seeking meaning, fulfillment, calmness, joy or hope. One's journey advances as one's life and efforts are meaningful, when one achieves communion with companions, God, and the world, and as one's self awareness is deepened and broadened. Each advance along the journey of our lives brings both a sense of completion or fulfillment *and* an awareness that the road still lies ahead.

Figure 11.1

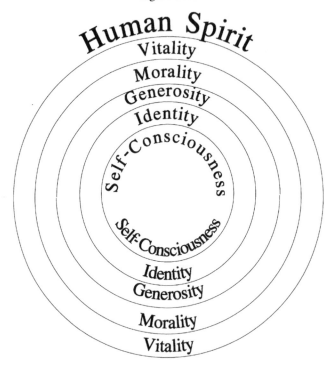

THE NESTED QUALITIES OF HUMAN SPIRIT

> Like an onion, human spirit is in layers. There is no
> essence that the layers or qualities enclose, but it is the
> qualities themselves that form spirit. The health of
> one's spirit reflects the state of the six qualities. We use
> several other words for this spirit: "self," "soul," "me,"
> and "I."

The value of the journey is not in some ultimate destination, but in the
quality of the travel. The fulfillment of the journey is not a place but a state of
being. It is a way of being wherein one's self rests complete for a spell. Paul
Tillich called those completed moments an experience of the "Eternal Now"
when past and future recede, displaced by the abundance of the present.[1]
Like any state of being, these moments of completion host learnings and
resources that can serve for a lifetime. The *state* of being, however, is tempo-

rary. No cognitive or emotional condition can last for very long unless there is some cognitive or emotional breakdown. It is the normal condition that our state of being is dynamic and temporary.

The natural rhythm of the development of meaning looks something like this: disquiet sends us searching, searching leads us to struggle, through struggle we discover meaning, with meaning comes a sense of completion and rest, and in the rest we are empowered for the next question and search. This meaning-making tactic gives our lives a spiralling quality as we pile meaning upon meaning like the coils of a spring. It is the nature of growth that the rest of understanding has to be achieved over and over again as our experiences and needs accumulate.

With each completion new avenues are revealed, opening the paths to still another level of completion. It's this periodic completion or rest of one's self that energizes life. It's not the rest of a contented cow. It is the "rest" of one's spirit that is at the core of a person who, to paraphrase the scripture from Isaiah, is able to run and not be worn out, to take off with the strength of an eagle, and to walk and not grow weak. That kind of experience only happens with a calm spirit.

To be sure—to quote an anonymous little poem—

> There are people who creep into the world to eat,
> To sleep and know no reason why they
> Are born, but only to consume the
> Corn, devour cattle, fowl and fish,
> And leave behind an empty dish.

And it is possible to avoid the journey, and still be counted as among the living. But for most of us, it is simply not enough to just breathe and eat. We want some kind of engagement with life that reveals truth and meaning, not simply a foggy existence devoid of trouble. Theologian-psychologist Harvey Potthoff expressed it this way:

> To experience one's self as a person growing in integrity and a sense of personal worth, and in sensitive involvement in the world of persons and events, is to experience the blessedness of being a human being.2

When our journey doesn't lead to that kind of experience, then we experience an alienation that is probably the most dreaded pain that exists. To us, when our soul or spirit goes flat, as Edna St. Vincent Millay describes in the last stanza of her poem *Renaissance,* the sky will and does "cave in on us by and by." The cave-ins usually happen when fear, grief, guilt, depression, anger or hate reduces our life stories to bad dreams.

Religion in our life gives us an inner life that seeks those meanings that enlarge our spirits, deepen our awareness, and reconnect us to God and neighbor.

PILGRIM

I want to return to the work of the late anthropologist Joseph Campbell. In his book *The Hero With a Thousand Faces*, Campbell described a myth found in most cultures of the world about this journey (see Figure 11.2). It is told differently in its detail from place to place, but all the versions carry the same universal theme. The stories are about one who hears a call from outside the bounds of the lifeless or threatened village. It is a call to break free of the village confines and to embark on a search for a new but hidden truth that will transform the village into a paradise and bring the pilgrim into communion with the heart of things. The one who hears and responds to the call becomes "Hero" or "Pilgrim."[3]

All the stories tell of a hero's risk-taking to discover the needed cure for the villagers: risks that are part of the very nature of the quest. The journey starts as an adventure, but soon Pilgrim must do battle with demons and forces that are foreign, and endure the deep loneliness of being far from home.[4] The hero overcomes the "dungeons of the mind" in time to discover the boon the home village needs. Pilgrim even encounters the Source of the saving boon—an encounter of such force and significance that Pilgrim is transformed into a new person dedicated to delivering the boon to the village.[5]

Pilgrim returns home with that which is needed only to meet opposition. This struggle with the old provincialism of the village proves to be the most challenging struggle of all. Yet, because of Pilgrim's new strength, self-awareness and grace, even this struggle is overcome and the village is transformed.[6]

Our cognitive and spiritual journey that begins at birth is like this myth. The myth is a life-metaphor: Sometimes we find ourselves stuck in a rut—a village. Within the sameness of village, there comes a call to go forward into fresh life and a new adventure. But to set forth to find a freshness and vitality to living is to encounter conflict and to engage in battle. It also means that whoever answers the call will have to endure loneliness and the strong urge to return to the comfort of "home."

If we are able to keep our faith in the call to move forward and refuse to shrink back into life's womb, there is the promise of escape from the dungeons of dread and fear and the hope of an encounter with what is holy, life-

Figure 11.2

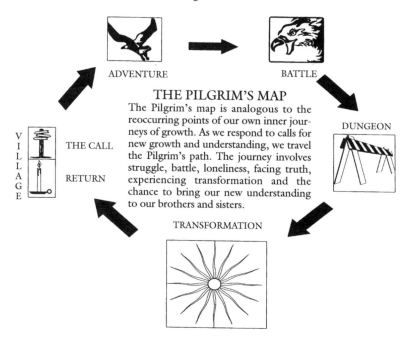

ADVENTURE   BATTLE

VILLAGE   THE CALL   RETURN

DUNGEON

TRANSFORMATION

THE PILGRIM'S MAP
The Pilgrim's map is analogous to the reoccurring points of our own inner journeys of growth. As we respond to calls for new growth and understanding, we travel the Pilgrim's path. The journey involves struggle, battle, loneliness, facing truth, experiencing transformation and the chance to bring our new understanding to our brothers and sisters.

changing and redemptive. This encounter so changes us that we become the bearers of it to our kin who have yearned for the same freshness that called us out into the wilderness. Imagine each of the segments of Pilgrim's journey as metaphors of our own spiritual journey.

The Village

We have to begin every new episode of our lives from some *matrix* (a word which comes from the Latin for "womb" or "mother"). We begin our lives with a very simple matrix of meaning, hopefully consisting of experiences of nurture and trust. This "mothering matrix" is meant to be a launch site for new meanings and experiences rather than a stage for rehearsing old ones. So, from our first conclusions about life, we are urged on to more sophisticated ones. Each growth of understanding means leaving an old matrix, an old "village." When we become too comfortable and too much at home with what was, then the matrix, or village, of thought, action, relationships or habits begins to deaden us. And since every cognitive leap and meaning leap, every change in the models we use to engage life, mean leaving, dying, and forsaking a part of ourselves, many of us do not easily grow.

Fortunately, there is an itch in us that will not tolerate sameness too long. It is a cognitive program that we are born with. It makes us ache to hear some news of another way of living or thinking that will add meaning to our days, answers to our questions and novelty to our routines. So, to each of us in those terrible itchy moments, there seems to come an invitation or call to leave the routine. It comes in the form of a witness of one who has "returned," the lure of "pinnacles" that we can barely see from the uneasy place where we stand, or from a nagging within—but from somewhere there comes a call to go forward. This is the urge to grow. It does not have to be taught, but we can be taught to squelch it.

The Journey

Whether from boredom, itchiness, or from being enticed by a call from outside the walls of the village, when we make up our minds to go, it becomes for us a great ADVENTURE. To leave old moldy ways of being is exhilarating. There is in the leaving a joy, freedom and anticipation of the next turn and the next day. Some new pursuits that we embark upon are more exciting than others, but there is no mistaking the feeling that the deadness of the village is gone. Novel ideas, information, and experiences are naturally pleasant to us. Learning and discovery activate a part of the hippocampus that gives us the experience of pleasure.

But there is another side to the new adventure. No one can leave from a matrix and avoid the onslaught of what seems like attack. If we leave some comfortable belief, there will be protests and warnings from those with whom we once believed. There will be protests from our own memory that cannot see a new integrity. When we leave conventional models, mores and morality to express our own ethical understanding, we meet protest and opposition within and without. To seek a new way is to do battle with the powers that avoid change. In the midst of such inner conflict, finger-wagging and attack, we are tempted to turn back and limp home. Still the call forward sings to us, and if we are able to hold fast, somehow we are pulled on through.

Perhaps the most unbearable part of the journey comes when we feel so far from what we think of as the normal way of acting and thinking that the journey's purpose evaporates under the heat of fear. It is the part of our pilgrimages when loneliness, dread and anguish become too much. In these times, the call forward to a fresh uncovering of our human nature and purpose seems so far off that we wonder why we ever left home. It is as dark as a dungeon. Learning and growth has this aspect too: self-doubt, dread, alienation and worry, as well as the experience of exhilaration and adventure.

In the dungeon, keeping faith is the single most important task. It is the one who has been endowed with courage and hope (gifts, strangely enough, from the village) who does not give up on the call that can barely be heard. It is the one who remains faithful that emerges from the dungeon at the threshold of a transformation.

The fundamental article of faith for the pilgrim is this: there will be an answer to questions of purpose and meaning and it will make all the difference. The pilgrim believes that every journey will give up its secrets and that he or she will be renewed.

The moment of insight and discovery may not be a burning bush with God's voice giving direction (but it might), and it may not even be what one really expected (but it might). In fact, the moment of insight and encounter with elusive and holy presence that sheds light on self and world might come while sitting on a park bench, while milking a cow, during the downing of a beer or in the embrace of someone you love. No matter on what shape of mountain we encounter that which transforms us, it is nonetheless a holy encounter that radically reshapes our models, our meanings, our manifesto, and our matrix of being.

There's no one who hasn't been given an insight or truth that can be redemptive to somebody else. Everyone has a word to speak to the village, a manifesto to proclaim. Often it is hard to share because it is disturbing or demanding. Still, the village needs it. It needs each person's word spoken personally and not as an edict or pronouncement. It needs us as the incarnation of what we have discovered from our journeys of meaning.

Returning the boon to the village means being our truth within the matrix from which we launched our search.

Pilgrimage is a deeply religious idea. The stories of Abraham's journeys, Moses and the burning bush, Adam and Eve leaving Eden, Gautama Buddha's path to enlightenment, Paul's Damascus road experience, and Jesus' journey to the cross—all of these stories share the pilgrim motif. It is part of human culture and psyche. I recommend it as a model for life because it serves to connect us with those who have traveled before, because it helps to order our secular lives in a way that points to a clear connection with the sacred, and because it makes more sense to think of God as that which calls us forward than as a security within which to hide. In addition it is a functional metaphor for the development of memory and meaning made possible by the chemistry, circuitry and biology of the brain.

FOUR LIFE-SCRIPTS

In Sophocles' play *Oedipus Rex,* the menacing Sphinx challenged Oedipus with a riddle: "What walks on four legs in the morning, two legs at noon and three legs in the evening?" the Sphinx asked. "Answer it correctly," it taunted, "and the ancient city of Thebes will be rid of my tyranny. Its people will again know the fullness of life." Oedipus, in a flash of insight, answered, "A human being! We crawl at birth, we walk upright at maturity, and in old age we use a walking stick." The Sphinx committed suicide and Thebes was saved.

Much of life is a riddle to us. We get clues and hunches about the mysteries of living, but now and then our hunches coalesce into powerful perspectives, ones that evaporate old problems and liberate ideas. Such is the power of high fidelity perspectives, ones that come very close to the elusive truth.

The conviction that people are beings on a journey of growth from birth to the grave is one of those high fidelity perspectives. It is a point of view that can liberate our ideas and expectations, even our very lives, so that we can get on with the task of living abundantly. The Pilgrim model has high fidelity.

Perhaps a way to grasp the value of the Pilgrim model is to look at some of its alternatives (see Figure 11.3). One alternative might be called the "Potter Model." This perspective is built on the belief that full humanity can be achieved with the proper training, molding and firing. It is founded on the conviction that during this trial we call living there will be forces molding our spirits. To accept this perspective is to believe that the world is a spiritual proving ground where suffering is designed to weed out weaklings and toughen the faithful into righteous pots.

Religious education based on this belief is marked by its emphasis on training, behavior modification and conformity to the norms of the teacher/potter. The potter shapes the clay while it is wet and malleable, and one day it will become a hardened vessel. To get a useful pot means the clay has to be shaped from the outside. The clay itself is powerless to contribute to its own being. At a certain stage it must be glazed and fired to become a full-fledged pot.

The "trial" (potter) model is a passive experience for the student who is being conditioned for life. It emphasizes personal perfection and educates followers to be good and obedient. This perspective ignores the fact that people grow through stages of moral development and religious insight. Instead, this style of education teaches people to believe right doctrine and to behave in ways worthy of the religious tradition. In the final analysis, this point of view makes the world a cruel place and puts people in the crossfire between the forces that seek to mold their being. In the social sciences, this is the approach of the behaviorists.

A second perspective is that of the "ascent to adulthood." It is a point of view that thinks of the time of childhood and adolescence as periods of ordeal one must endure in order to become a full person: an adult. This per-

Figure 11.3

FOUR LIFE-SCRIPTS

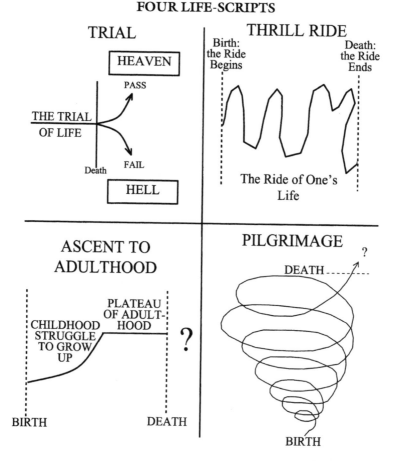

spective is founded on the belief that the goal of life is to grow up and live happily ever after. This is the perspective I swallowed along with my Ovaltine as a child. I still find myself wondering why I am not living as happily ever after as I was led to believe I would.

According to this model, the world is an overpowering place for children. Attachment to skillful and manipulative adults is essential for their future. Parenting and education are a matter of overwhelming children with what adults know they need, ignoring what the children want. It is a world where children are nonentities. This point of view takes seriously the belief that we grow through stages of physical and emotional development, but assumes that the developing child is not capable of contributing to his or her educational agenda since he or she is not yet fully human.

This model is a step closer to the pilgrim perspective in that there is a hint of life as journey, but it fails to affirm that the whole life span falls within the boundaries of the pilgrim's map. This is the developmental perspective of the Freudians.

My father's experience in Alcoholics Anonymous is an example of the limits of this perspective. I remember when he received his ten-year "chip" for sobriety. Ten years before, after a car crash, jail and attempted suicide, he was ordered to a treatment center and then started AA. Dad was sixty at the time. He told me that the hardest part of his ordeal was not jail or the humiliation he felt after reading the police report of the incident in his hometown paper. Rather, it was the demands of the twelve-step program in AA. "I had to start all over," he told me. "Here I was sixty and I had to learn to walk again. I thought of myself as a grownup for most of my life, and those AA guys were telling me to grow up." "Son," he said to me, "I feel more like a child now than I did when I was ten. But I am beginning to love nearly every minute of it." Dad had bought the model of "the ascent to adulthood" in order to attain the life change that his AA brothers and sisters helped him to. From then till his death, he knew himself as a pilgrim.

The third script is what I call the "thrill ride." Here we have a point of view that hinges on the belief that faith and feeling must coincide. What is real is what is felt, and feeling precedes faith. The object of faith and trust is that which brings excitement, calm, love, victory—even fear and sorrow. If I feel alive, loved, connected, and happy, my spiritual life must be fine. If I experience too long a period of dread, doubt and pain in my life, something must need fixing. This perspective assumes that the job of the religious leaders and educators is to keep the hope alive that, in this emotional roller-coaster existence, God and my faith community will make me feel good. It evaluates a person's spirituality in terms of one's emotional tone. The goal of ministry built on this perspective is to get people to feel good, happy, warm, excited or at peace.

Don't get me wrong, there is definitely an emotional side to one's faith and belief. After all, feelings are our vital signs, so to speak, and alert us to our inner life, but when they become the reason for doing ministry, our work looks more like a cheap-thrills operation than an outpost for pilgrims.

The "pilgrimage model" is a corrective to these three low-fidelity perspectives. I am convinced that it can revitalize ministry. Adopt it and it will release the work of educators as if it were Thebes being released from the threat of the Sphinx. It is the point of view that makes the human life cycle central to the way we conceive of ministry. It is founded on seven affirmations:

1. Every human being, regardless of age or health, is both fully human and has budding potential. There are not degrees of humanness, only stages of human life. By this affirmation we confirm the full humanity of all people.

Babies are born with the basic human agenda for finding meaning, participating in community and showing care that is the core of all our enterprises. That basic urge is etched in our brains from birth. We were not little nothings at birth waiting to be molded into human beings; we were born card-carrying people, hungry for meaning, culture and community. Our humanity is established by our neural pathways.

2. Every human being arrives on the planet with the plan for growth already outlined in his or her genes. The developmentalists tell us that the growth steps are determined by the complex plan crunched into every cell in our bodies.[7] And since all of creation is God's, the genetic code is in a real sense God's plan. Every cell in every child's body "knows" more about what is best for that child than any teacher or counselor. I don't mean that we don't have a lot to learn from each other, but I do mean that each of us is born "knowing" basically what to seek. No one knows more about what I need than I do. We can be taught to forget it, bury it, deny it and even hide it, but knowing what to seek was there to start with.

To be sure, the plan is but an outline. *We* create the details for ourselves in concert with the culture and people we allow to enter our world. Yet, this outline is a complete blueprint that allows for novelty, mystery and surprise, even as it grows in very familiar patterns. As religious educators, ours is the task of nurturing that growth, adding to it, challenging it and celebrating it, but not manipulating it like bonsai trees.

3. From first breath to last, we grow. There is no point in the life cycle when we can say the growth is finished—not physically, not emotionally, not intellectually and not spiritually. This is the testimony of developmental researchers like Eric Erikson,[8] Jean Piaget,[9] Lawrence Kohlberg,[10] and James Fowler,[11] and it is the testimony of four thousand years of human faith history.

4. Growth is sequential and generally predictable. For example: Erikson's description of eight stages of human growth asserts that each stage of psychological and social development happens **in a predictable order, and in certain times in a person's growth.** Piaget came to the same conclusion about cognitive development. When it comes to moral and religious growth, the pace may not be as predictable, but the sequence seems to be. There is plenty of discussion about the validity of certain models of human development, so we need to be open to fresh and less biased research about how people grow. Still, what all the research points to is that **we grow** and unfold

into what starts as potential. We become mature, intelligent and faithful people in a lifelong pilgrimage of emergence and discovery. We are not pots to be molded, but sacred organisms to be nurtured and challenged.

5. Growth in intellect, physique, emotion and spirit happens best in a particular kind of spiritual and social ecology, namely, the kind that feeds its creatures on justice, waters them with love and respect, and is cultivated by affection.

Imagine the isolation the Jews experienced when they were exiled in Babylon. Cut off from their community of faith and homeland, they languished. Consider further how they survived the ordeal because they were able to recreate that spiritual ecology in a foreign land. Such was the power of their community's ecology. Look to religious educators like C. Ellis Nelson,[12] Ross Snyder[13] and Paul Irwin[14] for in-depth descriptions of the formative power of spiritual ecologies.

6. Nurturing people in faith cannot be done the same way for all ages, cultures and personalities. Educating and worshiping require an extensive knowledge of human cognitive and emotional development—knowledge that will enable educators to tailor experiences to the needs, crises, aspirations and agenda of the community's pilgrims. We know now *empirically* what wise men and women have sensed for ages: that learning and faith transmission demands skill with words and pictures, logic and intuition, poetry and prose, story and lecture, action and stillness, symbols and direct experience—all in varying combinations as each human being's development requires.

7. Life-cycle ministry affirms that living is both cyclical, where patterns and decisions are made again and again, and directional, where novelty and growth are always a potential. Each of us is a pilgrim on a journey of discovery. In fact, we are on multiple journeys. And the pattern of the pilgrimage will be repeated throughout our days. But the pilgrimage cycle is no circle; it is a spiral of growth. We may fall off the spiral, get sidetracked or stuck, but the plan of God is that we grow on toward some kind of perfection. The "payoff," if you will, is not that people arrive at that perfection, but that along the journey life's fullness will be embraced, the companionship of the Holy One will be experienced and depth of community will be touched. The journey's the thing.

But what causes this growth along predictable stages? Organisms grow best in the company of an immense diversity of life. Life in a rain forest is possible because of the enormous variety of life in the forest system, not homogeneity. The same is true of people. Our worlds of meaning, our models of ourselves in creation, and our skills for living are enhanced by deeper and wider experiences. We gather in congregations that are spiritual ecologies, drawing meaning, support, and life itself from the variety of ages, conditions and backgrounds in the congregation. The more diverse, the better. In fact, the dynamo that moves a person along his or her journey through the stages of growth is diverse experiences, rich encounters and a growing stock of knowledge.

Children especially benefit from educational and cultural experiences that are cross-generational, multicultural, and interethnic. If our faith communities don't reflect the variety of humanity, then educators ought to arrange for these opportunities for the children outside the bounds of the congregation. Sadly, faith communities remain one of humanity's most homogeneous ecologies.

The point is, growth is a matter of accumulation. When a child first comprehends how the amount of milk in a glass remains the same when it is poured into a bowl (an ability that marks a child's movement from stage one to stage two in Piaget's model of cognitive growth), the jump in ability is a matter of accumulated experience, not a result of the child's age or some timer going off in the genes.

ELEVEN POINTS OF PILGRIM MINISTRY

What does life-cycle ministry look like? I suggest eleven marks of this kind of ministry. In Pilgrim Ministry:

(1) Attention is given to the implications of physical development. Our worship, educational, and recreational places reflect a sensitivity to the physical needs of toddlers, teens and centenarians, as well as able-bodied, middle-aged adults.

(2) Developmental differences are noted and taken into account in curriculum and planning. Methods and content reflect an understanding of developmental theory.

(3) People grow as they are drawn into deeper and wider appreciation for creation. So leaders and teachers are selected for their particular ability to move us along on our pilgrimages. Teachers and counselors are trained to call people forth more than thay are trained to pack their brains with information.

(4) Growth, crisis and redemptive moments are marked by celebrations. People intersect divinity daily. We can mark moments of insight and growth at the loss of the first tooth, a significant birthday, the recovery from an illness, loss of a loved one, marriage, graduation, retirement. Life-cycle ministry invents liturgies that help us celebrate those intersections.

(5) Pilgrim ministry emphasizes nurture over training. Training in skills

like prayer, worship and Bible study ought to be on our agenda, but always behind the concern for growth.

(6) Pilgrim ministry zeros in on crises as teachable moments. Remember that *crisis* can refer to a moment of risk *or* opportunity. Crises are turning points and can be experiential peaks (such as weddings, births or getting a job) or valleys (such as loss, conflict or boredom). Sermons, classes and newsletters will invite thinking and decisions related to occasions that push and pull us in new ways. One-on-one counseling with professionals and peers is made available for those who need it, affirming the redemptive power of life's duets.

(7) Programs are tailored to people's needs, age and interest. Programs tend to look like a smorgasbord of opportunities, content and settings.

(8) Nurture and teaching is done as often as possible as a whole community of faith, with all ages and many kinds of past experience represented.

(9) In order to build up this nurturing, redemptive ecology, our ministry presents the faith through story, liturgy, music and word in a concert of experience that will attract and nurture many different people. Words alone, music alone, the arts alone touch only a few. But when we multiply the media and methods by which we do ministry, we make it possible for people to worship, learn and share across the many cultural, experiential and developmental boundaries that make humanity interesting.

(10) Leaders look more like gardeners, midwives and player coaches than pruners, potters, doctors and managers.

(11) We are concerned that every human be blessed with a redemptive, nurturing ecology of spirit within which to flourish. Ultimately, we all share the same ecology. Life-cycle or pilgrim ministry, therefore, is passionately involved in the movement for justice and love for each member of the planet. And since no organism exists in isolation, we are concerned that justice and care extend to every life-form.

Martha Snyder wrote of an encounter between a student teacher and a four-year-old that speaks of the power of redemptive spiritual ecologies, the humanness of all ages, the surprises that can happen, and the naturalness of the human search for connection and meaning. It is so common an exchange that it could go unnoticed by most as the evidence of the power of the perspective of a small child.

At the beginning of the spring quarter, Tom, a new student teacher, came into the school for the first time. He had never had any experience with young children. Four-year-old Estelle noticed him sitting in the corner of the school yard looking very serious. Estelle went to him, touched his shoulder, came close to his face and spoke to him:

Estelle:	"Haven't you had any birthdays?"
Tom:	"Yes, I've had birthdays."
Estelle:	"Didn't your mother bake you cakes?"
Tom:	"Yes, my mother baked me cakes."
Estelle:	"And didn't she put candles on them?"
Tom:	"Yes, I had candles on my cakes."
Estelle:	"Then why are you so sad?"[15]

Life-cycle ministry expects God's love and justice to show up anywhere, through anybody, at any time.

Each of us is both a changeling and an integrity. Our lives are a succession of clearings and transformations, but the one who moves through those changes would remain "you" or "me." Over time the "me" I have always been has grown and accumulated a universe of meaning. We Pilgrim Minds grow in communities of minds where we meet each other in authentic soul-to-soul exchange. Growth is the reward. Martin Buber said, "All real living is meeting."[16] Perhaps he would consent to a corollary: all real meeting accumulates to help us grow.

CHAPTER TWELVE

The Emergence of Consciousness

DASEIN

I HAVE ARGUED that our brains are physically designed to make us cognitive and spiritual changelings headed toward wider and deeper awareness of ourselves, others and our worlds of meaning. We are expansive. We model the world with data constantly being arranged in our brains. As the models develop, they come to include a model of ourselves. One of the incredible results of the expansion of the universe within us is the gradual emergence of an **awareness** of that self-model. It is this emerging awareness of self that makes possible (among other things) reflective thought, projected futures, story telling and conscious deciding.

According to Eric Erikson, this self-awareness blossoms and passes through a critical period during adolescence.[1] Apparently, our models of life (all ten levels of modeling referred to in chapter 2) have to reach a high degree of complexity and integration before identity and consciousness of self can take center stage. Typically, writes Erikson, it takes about twelve years to reach that complexity. Identity development remains center stage for as long as twelve more years before being upstaged by the need to develop the strong patterns of intimacy identity permits.

I began the previous chapter with a frame from my own biography. That moment matters in this discussion because it marks a point in my pilgrimage when I was just beginning this "identity crisis." I became aware of my own self as an integrity in process. I suspect all of us can recall similar occasions of awakening, especially during adolescence, when we beheld our own self. Perhaps this accounts for the large number of teens who report religious experiences and conversions that mark a rearrangement of and fidelity to lifelong values, manifestos and symbols.

I do not want to imply that people have no identity before they are teenagers; rather, I mean to say that it does not become a central agenda until those transitional years between about ages twelve and twenty-four.

152

Indeed, the formation of one's self gets underway immediately at birth and the person we are throughout our adulthood is to a large degree set in the first ten years.

Nor do I want to suggest that we are never self-aware *before* adolescence. At a very young age children are able to draw pictures of themselves, tell stories about themselves, imagine what others think of them and converse with themselves. Clearly, we get to work on creating a model of ourselves early in the life cycle.

Nevertheless, during adolescence the development of a person's self-model becomes central. What it seems to be "doing" on that stage is learning to behold itself. Remember how Descartes concluded that "I think, therefore I am!" In that vein, the teenager concludes "I think of myself thinking, therefore I am!"

When I had my epiphany on a Sunday afternoon at thirteen, I felt as though I had just awakened, had shaken the sleep from my eyes, and then was standing before myself. I was, as Karl Jaspers named the experience, *dasein*. The German word means "being there." Existentialists used the word to stand for "human being."[2] The term fits my experience. The self-aware person is aware of being there.

BUT WHAT IS CONSCIOUSNESS?

The fact that we can know of our being-here has prompted articles, books and research in cognitive science over the last three decades. One of the harder aspects of the research has been to define consciousness and self-awareness. For my purposes, **consciousness** refers to the experience of being aware of one's thoughts and experiences (what neuroscientists call *qualia*) so as to be able give a report of them to someone else. **Self-awareness** is that state of mental focus wherein you think of yourself, your thoughts, your experiences. You behold yourself.

We can focus our awareness on anything thinkable but focusing on ourselves thinking is not quite like thinking of anything else. It is a unique and powerful strategy for making meaning. It sits atop a ladder of liveliness and exists because of the levels beneath it. Each rung represents a new threshold in aliveness (see Figure 12.1).

At the bottom of this ladder is biological life. All living organisms participate in this level. It has one basic requirement shared by all the levels above it: the ability to interact with the environment.

Above that basic level is the level of alertness. Being alert implies that an organism can also be at rest. The rhythm between states of readiness and rest

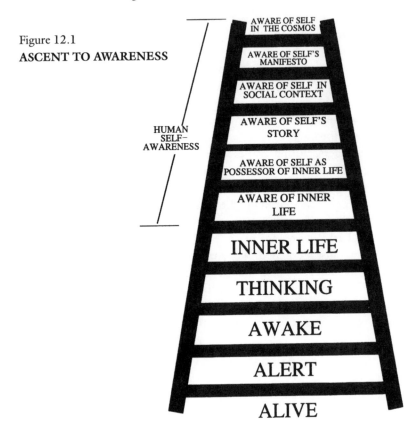

Figure 12.1
ASCENT TO AWARENESS

HUMAN
SELF—
AWARENESS

AWARE OF SELF
IN THE COSMOS

AWARE OF SELF'S
MANIFESTO

AWARE OF SELF IN
SOCIAL CONTEXT

AWARE OF SELF'S
STORY

AWARE OF SELF AS
POSSESSOR OF INNER LIFE

AWARE OF INNER
LIFE

INNER LIFE

THINKING

AWAKE

ALERT

ALIVE

can be seen in most animal organisms. Alertness is the state of being ready
for something to impinge. The environment around a single-celled animal or
a wolf can trigger automatic strategies that make them ready for special
response.

Just above that is the state of wakefulness. Being awake implies that an
organism can have a time of sleep or relative unresponsiveness to an environment. It took millions of years of evolution for sleep and wakefulness cycles
to emerge, and only animals with a relatively complex central nervous system
seem to do it.

Related to wakefulness, but more intense, is the ability to give attention.
It is a prerequisite to the next level and requires sharp and discerning senses
(especially hearing, seeing and smelling, the long-range or "tele-senses").

Next is the focus of attention to problem solving. In lower animals
almost no problem solving goes on because their nervous system includes
behaviors that are initiated automatically as they encounter certain stimuli.

But in higher vertebrates that have enough cortex to allow information to be gathered and put to use, problem solving or "thinking" can happen. Although the problem solver may not be conscious of the process, the cortex is able to gather and evaluate information and initiate appropriate behavior.

Along with problem solving, this level of aliveness includes the ability to have more complex emotions beyond states of alert and calm. Fear, excitement, anger, depression and pleasure can be identified in but a few species of animals and almost all of them are mammals. The larger the cortex in relation to the rest of the animal's brain, the more subtle and varied are its emotional states. The development in evolutionary history of the ability to have emotions and sensations (like physical pain and pleasure) laid the ground work for the experience of an inner life. This seems to be the exclusive property of primates.

The next rungs are (apparently) the exclusive property of Homo sapiens and properly belong to the category "self consciousness." They include:

> Our awareness of our thoughts and inner state (we know what we are thinking and feeling), along with a sense of choice about actions made related to the objects of our conscious thoughts;
> Our awareness of ourselves;
> Our awareness of ourselves as the possessor of and main actor within a stream of conscious thoughts and a lifelong story;
> Our awareness of ourselves within a physical, social and spiritual ecology; and
> Our awareness of our manifesto among others and against the backdrop of the universe.

Cognition done at lower "rungs" of aliveness are processes we do not choose; rather, they result from the pandemonium of mental activity that accumulates to produce routine, unconscious behavior. The last rungs, however, represent the levels of aliveness that allow the self to choose behavior. The possibility of cognitive freedom rests at these last levels of aliveness. To act with freedom and to make moral choices are reserved for these last levels. Henry David Thoreau put it more to the point: "Moral reform is the effort to throw off sleep."[3]

Social philosopher Alfred Schutz called this highest of human consciousness "Wide-Awakeness." He wrote:

> By the term "wide-awakeness" we want to denote a plane of consciousness of highest tension originating in an attitude of full attention to life and its requirements. Only the performing and especially the working self is fully interested in life, and hence, wide awake. It lives within its acts and its attention is exclusively directed to carrying its project into effect, to exe-

cute the plan. This attention is an active, not a passive one. Passive attention is the opposite of full awareness.[4]

Because so much of what we call "religious" life happens or is developed in our self consciousness, to be able to nurture, strengthen, widen and broaden consciousness in students is central to our work as educators. As we understand the phenomenon more fully, we will get clues about the nurturing, strengthening, broadening and widening of consciousness in general.

HOW IS SELF-AWARENESS AND CONSCIOUSNESS EVEN POSSIBLE?

A pattern is emerging from among researchers about the origins of consciousness and self-awareness. Here are some of the conclusions:

1. Self-awareness and consciousness are "points" along a consciousness continuum (see above).[5]
2. Consciousness, self-awareness and spirit cannot come into being without the brain. They may outlast it, but the brain is their birthplace.[6]
3. However, self-awareness and consciousness is not generated by a specific area of the brain; rather, it is made possible by several brain areas and cognitive programs interacting. It happens after a certain level of cognitive complexity is achieved. It is like the harmonies, overtones and chords that are created when individual musical notes are played at once.[7]
4. The self is that which seems to experience consciousness and use consciousness and is the "central meaner," that which claims what we are conscious of.[8] I am being metaphorical here. The self isn't a thing that has physical properties. It is the *meanings that we are* that claims or "owns" the thoughts we are aware of.
5. The self is the "gatherer" of biographic memory. I'm being metaphorical again. I mean that the events that the "Jerry" organism remembers are all connected by this self-model that I am. The self is the appreciator and valuer of that biography.[9]
6. The content of our consciousness *seems* like a portion of a stream of experiences which include: real time experiences of the physical world, inner thoughts, feelings, imaginings and recollections. This stream flows from as far back as our memories reach. Its integrity is maintained by the self that claims it all as "my story."
7. Phenomenologically the self is the observer of our conscious awareness. It has a "point of view," an observation position in our imagination.

8. The product of consciousness is *thoughts* we have about what and how we are thinking and experiencing, in addition to thoughts of the objective, physical world. We think about our perceptions. It only *seems* as though those thoughts are about what is really "out there."
9. These thoughts about ourselves, our inner representations of the world and our inner experiences of the world, are specific to each of us. All of the thoughts together, as they come and go through a day and over the years, accumulate to be who we are. In a sense we are a work-in-progress—made up, immaterial, a virtual reality being "constructed" of the meanings and story of a life.[10] The self remains the same self over time even as it grows and is transformed. However, it is not always "there." It is a potential called into play many times in a day as it is needed. It is conjured by the brain, processing information and making decisions that require mediation, resolution or judgment. Whenever I think "What will I do next?" my self is summoned (see Figure 12.2).

In summary, most of our actions, thoughts and perceptions get processed without our being conscious of them. They get processed in a sort of "pandemonium (to use D. C. Dennett's metaphor) of simultaneous cognition."[11] Consciousness happens when the self is needed or made to pay attention to some aspect of this fast-paced multiplicity of our brains. It can happen in at least four basic ways:

1) when the pandemonium fails to resolve a problem and we are stumped;
2) when we are aroused or alerted by strong feelings;
3) when we are "summoned" by an outside source (someone calls our name; we recognize a face or situation); and
4) when a strong memory is snagged by some experience.

Regardless of how consciousness is invoked, these things begin to happen:
1) attention is focused,
2) cognition slows down,
3) thoughts are thought about,
4) one's *self* seems to take control,
5) memories are gathered,
6) parts of the brain used to *do* the concentrated thinking begin to produce synchronous electrical pulses of 40 cycles per second,
7) we rehearse possibilities, imagine alternatives, and
8) our vital signs rise.

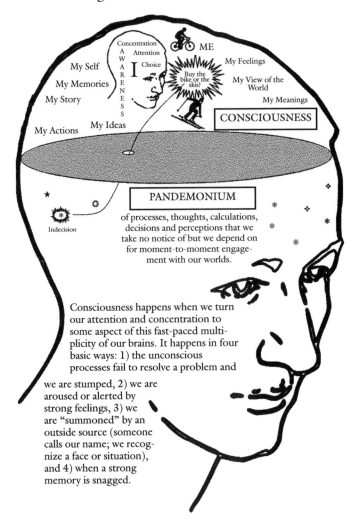

Concentration
AWARENESS
Attention
ME
My Self
I
Choice
My Feelings
My Memories
Buy the bike or the skis?
My View of the World
My Story
My Meanings
My Ideas

CONSCIOUSNESS

My Actions

Indecision

PANDEMONIUM

of processes, thoughts, calculations, decisions and perceptions that we take no notice of but we depend on for moment-to-moment engagement with our worlds.

Consciousness happens when we turn our attention and concentration to some aspect of this fast-paced multiplicity of our brains. It happens in four basic ways: 1) the unconscious processes fail to resolve a problem and we are stumped, 2) we are aroused or alerted by strong feelings, 3) we are "summoned" by an outside source (someone calls our name; we recognize a face or situation), and 4) when a strong memory is snagged.

Figure 12.2

What results from our consciousness and self-awareness might be a decision, an action, a conclusion, an experience of meaning and feeling, a creation, a destruction, or a pleasure. Whether something "punches" through from the pandemonium to our awareness or we are called by another person, our consciousness, and the self that seems to direct it, is assembled fresh each time.

HOW DID CONSCIOUSNESS
COME INTO BEING?

The need to *survive, find meaning* and *reproduce* are at the base of all our behaviors. Consciousness, like all of our abilities, evolved from these needs. Here's how it probably came into being.

Every organism "seeks" to survive. For mobile creatures such as you and me to survive, a "knowledge" of our living space is essential. To be able to recognize our world requires a point of view, and a point of view means that we can identify "inside" and "outside," "me" and "not me." This is important, not only to keep safe from harm or attack, but to relate us to our own kind upon whom we depend for so much. Every creature has to be able to recognize "me" and "not me," "mine" and "not mine."

For all animals throughout evolution, recognition of "me" and "not me" has been necessary in order to move about in their environment, identify food, mate and avoid danger. Vertebrates have evolved an elaborate array of senses to search and discover the nature of the "not me." What they discover informs them about moving, foraging, hiding, socializing, and so on. In a primitive way animals are always "asking": Where am I? What is that? and What do I do now? The "answer" to the last question for all mobile organisms is either "Scram," or "Go for It."

The more complicated the organism, the larger its repertoire for "scramming" or "going for it." After some new thing, shape, smell, sound, or the like, enters an organism's brain, and prior to its decision to run or approach, the whole organism's neural network revs up. Its senses update the situation, allowing the brain to lay down information that will tip it to action. This is the animal precursor to consciousness. This is not yet self-awareness, but it is close.

In evolution, regular heightened states of vigilance led some mammals to explore and acquire information long before needs arose and action was necessary. They became curious. Our ancestors developed very mobile eyes, and heads that helped them satisfy their curious nature. We and our ancestors might be called the "informavores"[12]—always hungry to know our worlds.

This "curiosity feature" led to important physical developments in the brain. The fast "dorsal brain" (visual cortex) took over immediate visio-spatial computations and real-time safety and piloting duties. The slower ventral (front and top cortex) areas were the informavore brain's storing and organizing areas.[13] In primates, the functions spread further into the left and right cortex with its emerging specializations.

Up to this point the evolutionary changes happened genetically so that the better-adapted genes (genotype) produced a better-adapted animal (phenotype). The changes were prenatal. Once born, you had all you were going to have in the way of equipment and strategies for survival. With the higher primates, postnatal "evolution" became possible because the animals could *learn* new and unique strategies for survival and curiosity.

In other words, the brain developed a plasticity and adaptability allowing it to "evolve" *during* its lifetime. A particularly good learning or skill would be recognized by others of the population and be copied. If it was really useful, it was part of the "education" of later offspring. The more useful learnings actually speeded up the course of the group.

Following the evolution of tan expanded cortex, the hominids and pre-chimps branched in evolutionary history. Our large-brained ancestors were poised for the biggest leaps in cognitive development up to that time. Ironically, their brains were virtually identical to ours.

Accelerated by learned behaviors, the split nature of the cortex, and the fast calculations of the left rear cortex, our ancestors learned to talk. They didn't just signal, they named things. They didn't just associate a sound with an object, they invented vocabulary, used grammar, and told stories. From that time, language has dominated human history. Although the infant brain of today is physically identical to that of the first Homo sapiens babies, the child of today is given a whole new set of "software applications" that take advantage of the brain's "operating system," the most important being its native language. With that software, we are able to more effectively model our worlds and track the chronological features of it—and of us in it.[14]

Language was used as a means of summoning help and communicating information necessary for survival decisions. Our ancestors *spoke* to each other to get help finding food, water and shelter. Often, however, there would be no one around to hear a person's request. Language was used mainly as a means of summoning help and communicating information necessary for survival. So our ancestors spoke to one another about where to find food, water and shelter. When there was no one to speak to or consult, individuals developed the routine of talking to themselves. The individual's "self-request" had the same effect as someone else making a request or answering a question. Thus humans developed "inner speech."[15]

According to Julian Jaynes, as language developed and as tribes and families began to encounter other clans, early humans learned caution. They had to be careful about what they revealed of their needs to strangers. A needy stranger could be a threat to a clan just barely making it.[16] The result, says Jaynes, was that some of the wiser ones learned a sort of subvocal inner or self speech to rehearse what they would reveal to others first. They learned to imagine talking through a possible plan of action *to themselves*. They would talk to themselves about the consequences of interaction with strangers and even make up a lie in order to survive. In the process, they had to invent a model of themselves which they could move around in their mental landscape to "do" the rehearsing. In addition, they "watched" the rehearsal, evaluating the possibilities. You can't do that without a self, a "me" or an "I" in your imagination.

In both cases (talking to yourself and rehearsing encounters), "inner speech" or reflective thought was the result. Jaynes claims that reflective thought and thinking about one's self was not possible until the development of language, intercultural travel and commerce.

Developing An "I"

So today, when we think, calculate and do problem solving, the thinking is done within the context of a history of memories and ideas attached to a accumulated sense of self. The "I" that is me has gradually taken shape as a concept and sort of metaphor of that which has been Jerry for fifty-five-plus years. When I consciously survey my world, become aware of my thinking—and even behold this self I have accumulated—I become, I am conscious of self.

Self-consciousness, however, is not just thinking, but also having an awareness of thoughts and thinking. The awareness occurs when something we think of causes heightened emotions, attentiveness and/or confusion. It is rather like waking up and glimpsing our selves in action. Over time the glimpses are recalled as a stream of consciousness.[17] This stream gets organized into a personal narrative we can tell to others. It could not happen without language and relationships. Helen Keller's blindness and deafness made language and relationships all but impossible for her until Annie Sullivan became her teacher. With Annie's help, teenaged Helen discovered herself and the people who loved her. The key was Annie's genius at giving Helen language. Keller wrote:

> Before my teacher came to me, I did not know that I am. I lived in a world that was a no world. I cannot hope to describe adequately that unconscious, yet conscious time of nothingness. . . . Since I had no power of thought, I did not compare one mental state with another.[18]

Self thinking is a kind of miraculous loop of thought wherein we think about us thinking, or acting, or being.[19] When we are able to make a loop in our thinking so that we examine our selves in our stream of consciousness, we are self-aware. It happens as a result of the interplay of human relationships, language, metaphorical thought—and after accumulating enough experiences to make the loop. Consciousness and self-awareness requires some specific skills and experiences:

- To be self-aware requires *concentration* on a task or decision so that we can bring into play logical processes that override automatic strategies of the subconscious. In other words, as we are able to concentrate attention, resources and options in memory, we enable consciousness. To be self-aware requires concentration on the tasks we are doing, the memories that are relevant, and the sensations that keep us in touch with the world. Lose your concentration, and you lose self-awareness.
- To be self-aware requires *the ability to access memory and meanings on purpose.* It requires self-knowledge, a considered life, and an active mind that can decide to be self-aware.
- To be self-aware sometimes requires *the ability to rehearse one's actions and decisions* before making or taking them. It means being able to imagine a condition, situation or outcome. It might require us to imagine a plan before it is implemented, a consequence prior to its causes, or a possibility before it can come about. The more we know of the world, the better will be our rehearsals. The bigger the picture of creation we can include in our conscious considerations, the more reliable will be our rehearsals.
- To be self aware requires "*inner speech.*" Inner speech is the dialogue that is carried on between "me" and the model of "me." I imagine myself and talk things over with myself. It can have the same range of depth, respect and clarity that we show in interpersonal speech. For those who do it best, it is honest, skeptical, probing and affirming. We are affected by what we tell ourselves as much as we are affected by what others tell us.
- To be self-aware requires *strategies for recall and inner speech that address all our seven intelligences,* including doodling, singing, playing, sculpting, pacing, visual search strategies, working, writing and reading. All these expressions can deepen and broaden self-awareness.

WHAT ARE THE FEATURES
OF SELF-AWARENESS AND CONSCIOUSNESS?

Stay with me a bit longer. I promise to get back to earth and the point for religious education soon. I hold stubbornly to the conviction that if we nurture and tend to souls, then we ought to know all we can about the science of soul-raising. When science can show us a way into that understanding, we had better pay attention.

Earlier in this chapter I mentioned Julian Jaynes. In a landmark book called *The Origins of Consciousness in the Breakdown of the Bicameral Mind,*

Jaynes describes the connection between the growth of human civilization and the development of self-awareness.[20] He brought together anthropology, history, literature, cognitive science, and philosophy to make the case that self-awareness is as young as five or six thousand years, having developed just after the rise of towns, cities and commerce. When people began to make contact with strangers and travelers, they soon found it was wise to be cautious. For their own well-being, Jaynes theorizes, early humans had to imagine themselves in situations of unfamiliar and risky social encounters prior to making contact. They would mentally rehearse the interaction, imagining themselves in that future encounter. One could not imagine that contact without having a model of oneself to practice on. Thus began the development of self-awareness.[21]

There are six features of self-awareness, according to Jaynes, that we have come to nurture in each other with our language, stories, and culture.[22] We still depend on those features.

First, Jaynes says that our conscious awareness is organized *spatially* rather than sequentially. What we attend to (whether it is a memory, a book, speech, sounds, sights or different combinations) gets "placed" in our thoughts in the same spatial way they seem to exist in the world that we sense. If we have to attend to a lot of things, they get strewn around our virtual world. We consciously go from thought to thought like turning from scene to scene in a play, or page to page in a book. Russian psychologist Alexander Luria reported a case of a patient that points to the "landscape" nature of our conscious thoughts. The patient was plagued by a "photographic memory." Everything he committed to memory remained in his consciousness and crowded his thinking when he tried to interact with others. He was overloaded with things he felt compelled to attend to. The patient reported that, quite by accident, he had discovered a way to forget. He simply hid the unwanted information in his imagination. He put meaningless and unwanted memories of addresses and names behind imaginary trees and hung a conjured cloth over them. He put a person who kept popping up in his thinking into a shadow or somehow camouflaged that person. By using the spatial nature of consciousness he hid memories like Easter eggs.[23]

Related to the spatial nature of the landscape of consciousness is the second feature Jaynes called *excerption*. Excerption refers to the fact that what we are aware of is partial, as if it were seen from one angle at a time. One cannot think of a person's face and the back of the person's head at the same time. Our mental picture may shift quickly from one perspective to the other, but we do not normally hold them in our mind simultaneously. "Ah," you say, "but I can imagine the two views side by side." Yes, you can, and so can I. We can do it by imagining two people. But each of the imagined people will still be "seen" from a single perspective. As our senses receive only part of an experience, so our consciousness of what we sense or remember sensing is partial.

Third, says Jaynes, in that virtual reality called imagination there emerges an *analog "I"* that can move about, interact, explore, and experiment. It is through the "senses" of the analog "I" that we "experience" the virtual world. It is an analog of the integrity of our thoughts and history. It is the model of what Dennett calls the "central meaner," "the center of narrative gravity," the self. It is an analog of one's self.

Fourth, there is a *metaphor "me"* that we can "watch" do things in our virtual world. The analog "I" "watches" the metaphor "me." In a dream state, these two fictions come and go. We dream our dreams and then remember them as a story unfolding before us and then we ourselves seem to step into the picture and act.

Fifth, conscious moments (especially self-aware moments) are remembered as, and are part of, a personal *narratization* of our lives, an unfolding biography. Conscious experience is stored and recalled as a part of a narrative stream. Each episode, or moment of consciousness, is perceived as a picture or a scene, even a collage of scenes, but we recall them as or in a sequence.

Finally, Jaynes says that consciousness *conciliates* what we are aware of in order to eliminate as much ambiguity, dissonance, and lack of integrity as possible.

Religious thinking and being is at least wide-awake, conscious living. It is the mental state wherein a person is conscious of God, of one's relation to God, and one's being in creation. Consciousness and self-awareness are preconditions of being religious.

These six characteristics of consciousness can point to ways consciousness can be nurtured, strengthened, broadened and widened. They can be seen as teaching-learning strategies that can be included in a learning event in any of the points along the Spiral of Learning described in an earlier chapter. I believe that the points on the learning spiral themselves nurture consciousness, but there are some strategies that can be applied that will prove useful in nurturing self and consciousness. I present them in the categories suggested by Jaynes.

Spatiality

The spatial nature of our conscious thoughts is natural. When we think of what we are contemplating and experiencing, our awareness seems to be like a spotlight moving to the actors, props and scenery that have our attention. Or, it is like a desk or workspace we look over and then choose from it an item to attend to. This stage-workspace consciousness can be strengthened, making conscious thinking clearer.[24]

Diagraming with paper and pen is a way of spreading out ideas and experiences for conscious consideration. In chapter two (Figure 2.2) I used the Circus diagram to talk about the experience of "circusness." Encourage students to doodle or diagram their ideas and feelings. Try it yourself. Diagram fear. Use words, pictures, lines and figures to spread out before you the experience of fear—its causes, results, thoughts and memories. Any idea or feeling can be spread out like a diagram.

Or perhaps it can be drawn as a scene, or series of frames. It can be danced, acted, built and sculpted as well. Any spatial method of "spreading out" ideas, experiences and feelings will clarify them and give us another opportunity to be more deeply conscious and self-aware.

Excerption

Our conscious moments are always excerpted from a larger context. They seem to belong to a bigger picture. I recall a workshop I attended on parenting that might illustrate this. We were asked to imagine our children in their favorite place at home and then imagine what they were doing. I imagined seeing the place from the point of view of an adult standing at the back door of our house looking over at my sons building a skateboard ramp. I was annoyed as I imagined the scene because of the mess and noise their play caused. The leader of the workshop then asked us to imagine it again but from the perspective of the child, at their height, from their angle and from their experience. I was surprised at the difference in meaning a new perspective could provide. What they were doing seemed fun and important from the new perspective. By encouraging and leading us to report, reflect on, or recreate moments of meaning from several perspectives and angles, the leaders helped us to deepen and broaden our consciousness and discover meaning by sampling several *excerpts* from an event.

All our experiences are excerpts from a larger context. A story or experience gathers its meaning from its context, but we consciously experience only a piece at a time. We experience moments that are excerpted from something larger. In fact, we gather our self-image from the excerpts of living that we accumulate over the years. By telling our excerpted stories, we bring again to consciousness our selves even as we present our selves to others. By listening to each other's excerpts, our consciousness is deepened and widened because of being invited into another's stream of awareness. I can think of few more valuable gifts than this that one person can give another.

This is the theme of a beautiful book by psychiatrist-educator-author Robert Coles called *The Call Of Stories.* In it, Coles weaves a fabric of meaning and value by telling and reflecting on the stories he has come to know as a reader, listener, psychiatrist and educator. He writes:

> Stories are renderings of life; they can not only keep us company, but admonish us, point us in new directions, or give us the courage to stay a given course. They can offer us kinsmen, kinswomen, comrades, advisors—offer us other eyes through which we might see, other ears with which we might make soundings.[25]

When we take part in the rendering of another's story, our self models are permitted to jump into another's biographical or imagined story stream. To some degree we "live" the other's story, similar to living and remembering our own biographies. The telling and hearing of stories is an essential, powerful tool for deepening and broadening consciousness.

As students tell their stories (or draw them or write them), encourage them to tell them from unique perspectives. Suggest they tell their life histories from the perspective of a sibling, parent, or pet. They might want to video tape their own biography, make a mural of the events of a year, or display photographs of a period of transition.

When *you* tell stories, give different perspectives on the characters and locales by using pictures, artifacts, or role-playing. Your model will encourage students to imagine themselves walking around as some or all of the people in a story or experience. Fresh angles make a difference in the way people build their versions of stories and experiences. By doing this, they may pick up a new perspective for knowing and developing their own selves.

Just think how we have changed our thinking of the universe now that we have photographs and movies from space. Encourage students to reflect on and tell about their conscious lives from new points of view, seeing with the eyes of people different from themselves, and walking in the shoes of other pilgrims. It will raise their consciousness.

Analog "I"

We "look" at our conscious thoughts from our own "eyes." "Look" and "eyes" are in quotes because our eyeballs have almost nothing to do with the experience. The "one" who sees our thoughts is the self, a complex idea of us that represents the physical being now reading this book. That self, in fact, is really who we are. We can entice students into wider and deeper consciousness by encouraging self-reflection and inner speech.

Encourage students to refer to themselves. Pay attention to the number of times people refer to themselves. You may be surprised at the absence of first-person-singular referents. Encourage the use of diaries and poetry as personal disciplines of inner speech. Spend time talking about honest inner speech. That is, encourage students to have inner dialogues with themselves but ones that are totally honest. Encourage private prayer. Prayer is similar to inner speech, but the dialogue is between oneself and God. The similarity is that God does not stand before us like a friend, and so we need a metaphorical God in our minds to turn to. I am not implying that we just make up God, rather, that we somehow imagine God in our conscious landscape and aim our honest inner speech in that metaphorical direction.

Metaphor "Me"

Sometimes we think of and imagine ourselves. That sketchy image is the metaphor of who I am. We need that metaphor to plan, rehearse, practice and even to remember. It takes on the form and style of our selves, but can also be braver, meaner, kinder, stronger, and weaker than we actually are. It is hypothetical. It is a very useful creation. Encourage the image of that metaphor by suggesting that students draw it, write metaphors for it, display photos of each other, and fantasize about it. Not only will the use of a "me" deepen self-awareness, but it can be used to intentionally set personal goals and facilitate spiritual growth.

Narratization

Narratization and excerption are similar things. Narratization is always an excerpt. There is no other way to strengthen the ability to string one's life together in a story than to tell it. Our story is a sequence of events we can unreel. Like a film, our stories follow a main character (a "me") through encounters that reveal themes and motif. Let students tell their stories all kinds of ways. Invite them to act them, dance them, paint them, mold them, write them, cook them even! And in the process, don't forget to tell yours. We must model story telling.

Not only ought we to tell our own stories, we enhance consciousness by telling all manner of stories. Donald Miller, in his book *Story and Context*, reminds us of six components of story telling. If any of them are missing from the tale, the story is drained of some of its power. He writes that the story teller should self-consciously *stand within the story*, getting a feel for the tensions and potentials of it. Then, as the story gets told, he or she should *stand to one side* of it so as not to overpower the story with his or her own self. Third, the teller should narrate the story in a way that *keeps detail, feeling and meaning connected.* Fourth, he or she should *keep the tension of the story's drama* at the center of the telling. Fifth, the story needs to be *presented with a point of view about living in general.* Finally, the teller should seek to make the telling a *"word-event."*[26]

These components help engage the imagination of listeners and gets them to identify with others. Identification with someone else is an exercise in self-awareness, except that the analog "I" assumes another identity for a time. There are dangers in identifying with another too closely but those dangers are slight compared to having *no* chance to "walk in another's shoes." By skillfully telling our stories to each other, we flex our self-awareness in expansive ways.

Encourage students to put their stories in the context of larger narratives: their family, their cultural context—and within the great myths and rituals of their people that give their story meaning. Encourage them to be story collectors and to discover themes among various ethnic groups, in novels, movies and television stories. As people claim their stories in the context of the great themes of their people's story, they begin to see those themes in the events of each day. To nurture that skill is to make self-aware theologians.

Conciliation

Finally, explains Jaynes, being conscious means having an awareness of the contradictions, ambiguities and strangeness in one's life, and having the urge to conciliate or unify one's thoughts and meanings. Everyone's life story has elements and episodes that on the surface seem contradictory. Jaynes writes that being conscious will bring us face-to-face with ambiguity and contradictions. For some this is not a pleasant experience. It can discourage self reflection and deepening consciousness. Look for ways to encourage students to confront and deal with the contradictions, ambiguities and strangeness they encounter in what they are aware of, but within a safe, trusting community of care and respect.

Help students uncover the unity that underlies diversity and discontinuity. Invite a trusting group to tackle as a team a problem of ethics, religion and meaning. Each of us wants what we are conscious of to fit in some way in our world of meaning. We know that not everything will. There are solutions to many problems, but to others there is only mystery. Encourage students to make a place for mystery, wonder, indecision and incompleteness—even while urging them to discover continuity.

Nurturing awareness will nurture the student's self, strengthen character and durability, broaden the grasp of God's creation and deepen commitment to other selves. It is an essential task for religious pilgrims.

SELF AND RELIGION

Black Elk Speaks,[27] by John Neihardt, was recently produced as a play about the history of the Lakota Indians. In the play, Black Elk and his community tell the story of their people as they struggled for survival and meaning over the four hundred years of European dominance. Woven all through the story was the mythic background of the Plains Indians and their disciplines of spiritual consciousness. Their myths and rituals helped them to know themselves and maintain a link with the spiritual reality that they saw behind events. Their stories were like maps for their souls. Their spiritual disciplines were cognitive routines for creating states of consciousness and self-awareness that placed them in contact with the great themes and meanings of the Lakotas. These routines put them in a unique place of spiritual awareness and freedom. Even under the oppression of the Europeans, they could be free. Even in the face of death and terror, they had hold of a cosmic thread of meaning that helped them join in the creative "hoops" of meaning that structured their community life and personal biographies.

Black Elk's story reminded me that spiritual disciplines of prayer, meditation, worship, dance, singing, fasting, and work invoke consciousness. In consciousness we can choose among actions, character, principles, even emotional states. Our religious life (at its best) can serve as a ladder by which we ascend to levels of awareness and understanding that put our lives in durable and redemptive context.

Like Black Elk climbing a ladder to a meditation spot on a mesa, our religious life gives us access to meanings that harmonize our stories and lift them through the struggle for meaning into the light of conviction and belief. Like Black Elk's songs to the Great Spirit, our religious life can put us in touch with the creator and with our brothers and sisters soul-to-soul. Any conscious moment is an ascent to the place where selves can meet and grow.

Learning can go on without consciousness, but it is the learning of a robot. It is learning without the possibility of soul transformation. Conscious learning opens the way to the transformation and growth of one's self. Conscious learners and teachers need to employ the routines that invoke awareness. Maxine Greene calls this level of living "Wide-Awakeness."[28] Any other way of learning, she insists, is superficial. Story and ritual, religion and community are at the center of those routines. The glory and blessing of human nature is this gift: the ability to search for meaning and discover it, to manifest hopes and futures in the very things we do, to know one's self and be grateful, and to know something of what lies behind, beneath and above the sensed world.

To know that all this is possible because of protein, genes, nerve tissue, neurotransmitters and a whole lot of carbon is the astonishing fact cognitive science leaves us. It is this fact—that matter cradles spirit—which makes it possible for us to join Black Elk in his prayer to that which is at the heart of things:

> Great Spirit, lean close to the earth that you may hear the voice I send. You towards where the sun goes down, behold me; thunder beings, behold me; you where the summer lives, behold me! You in the depths of the heavens, an eagle of power, behold! . . . Great Spirit, my Grandfather, all over the earth the faces of living things are all alike. With tenderness have these come up out of the ground. Look upon these faces of children without number, and with children in their arms, that they may face the winds and walk the good road to the day of quiet. This is my prayer; hear me! The voice I have sent is weak, yet with earnestness I have sent it. Hear me! [29]

EPILOGUE

Duet

LIKE ANY CHARACTERISTIC of a species, self-awareness serves to improve our chances for survival and the survival of our offspring. Self-awareness requires that we know where "I" begins and ends. For humans, knowledge of physical and psychological boundaries are important for our survival as soon as we are conceived. We begin life connected with another human—our mother. At conception we begin to become a separate organism from mom and at birth we begin the work of separating from her.

Then, as each new person builds a sense of self, he or she embarks on a lifetime of relationships and separations that become a sort of rhythm to his or her personal stories. From the relationships we find and lose, make and break throughout our lives, we compose a sort of lifelong duet of connected but separate selves.

The one-to-one relationship is the cradle of our expanding consciousness. Sociologist Alfred Schutz[1] called this tandem a "we relation." It is within the "we relation" that we come to grow a self and an awareness of it. Schutz explains that when two people pay attention to each other and relate in present-tense awareness of each other, they are a growing organism. In the context of "we relations," both partners come to know themselves as a "me" living in companionship in a world that is home. I want to close this exploration of religious education and cognition with thoughts about the pivotal place of this essential "duet."

PHANTOM OF THE OPERA

My wife Linda and I went to see the production of *The Phantom of the Opera* at the Ahmanson Theater in Los Angeles a few years back. I slouched to the event with my lowbrow mentality expecting no more than an interesting afternoon. My expectations were way off the mark. I can only say that I am grateful for the darkness of the theater, for the climax of the story left me a sobbing mess. I was lured into such an identification with the Phantom—this murdering, manipulative creature—that in spite of his evil I recognized some of me in him. The story captured the power of the duet to form selves.

The Phantom was a man tormented by the isolation his deformed face forced upon him. Marked as subhuman, this horrible sight of a man with a beautiful voice and sharp intellect chose to participate in life as a phantom, a shadowy presence in the Paris Opera House, rather than in the open. To some he became an unseen tutor, to others he was a demanding critic or menacing presence, and to all the Phantom was a soul to reckon with, even to be feared. Accidents happened when he didn't get his way. Actors, dancers and singers were humiliated and frustrated by him, and there were those unexplained deaths.

From the vaults beneath the opera house, the Phantom planned his manipulations, pranks and tutoring sessions with young singers. Christine Daae was one he had nurtured from his guise as an unseen angelic tutor. The story revolves around his desire to possess her, love her and be loved by her, even as she is pulled to love someone else—Raoul.

All this took me into the second act in a detached mood. After all, it was simply a fresh setting for one of the oldest plots in literary history: the love triangle. Big deal.

Then, part way through the second act my psyche was snared. Christine, having seen the horror of the Phantom's face and the deeper disfigurement of his soul, realizes that he is the one who murders those who disappoint him and manipulates circumstances to get his way. And now he wants to possess her. In an emotional turnaround, Andrew Lloyd Webber, the creator of the musical production, peels away the hostility and the disappointment that animated the Phantom, allowing him to pour out his deepest cravings into a song. It was not a song pleading with Christine to make her life his. Instead, in a rare moment that opened like clouds parting, he sang his deepest desire:

> Say you'll share with me
> One life, one lifetime
> Lead me, save me
> From my solitude
>
> Say you want me
> with you
> Here beside you . . .
> Anywhere you go
> Let me go, too—
> Christine, that's all
> I ask of you. . . . (act II, scene 7)[2]

The clouds of rage could be kept back for only a moment, but it was long enough for his soul to shine unclouded. It was that simple line "Anywhere you go, let me go, too" that did me in. I cannot say for sure what happened to me except, in that moment, the actors and the composer opened me up, too. I knew the yearning ache he sang about—a passionate craving for someone important to me to say, "Come with me." As the Phantom sang, I felt it was I saying to my big brother when he went to deliver papers, "Jim, let me go, too." It was I asking my sometimes-too-busy dad, "Daddy, can I go with you?" Too many times I remember Dad saying no. I felt it was I unfolding my most recent map of the world and my fifth-grade teacher saying, "I'll look at it later." It was my son asking *his* too-busy dad, "Let me go, too." Or it was my daughter asking me to be present to her and my ignoring her need. How many times have I said no?

The Phantom had spoken a true thing about all of us: that among the few fundamental needs that motivate us, there lies the need to live with another and to travel as a companion a little way with them. We seek not simply to belong to some crowd or tradition, but to be related to one person at a time, to be with them, to go a ways in their presence, glad for the chance to reach across the gap that too easily widens between human beings. The Phantom was not just singing about the need to be intimate with someone of the opposite sex; he sang of the more fundamental requirement to travel alongside a friend, to occupy a special place in his or her world, as they do in his own, even if for a short time, and, in traveling with another, to come to know one's self.

The Redemptive Tandem

It is as if human life were really meant to be a duet. We may have a circle of friends, but we can relate deeply to but one at a time. Yes, for part of our lives we sing with a chorus, to press the metaphor, but it is within the duet that we sing our best. In fact, much of the evidence about the brain programs that we Homo sapiens come into the world with, indicates that they are designed to keep us related. Babies are born hungering to find a face, to meet eyes, and even to resonate empathetically with the contentment and distress of others. We are born ready to relate. Some have speculated that since living starts with the most intimate pas de deux between mother and unborn child, the ejection into separateness at birth marks the beginning of the lifelong pilgrimage wherein we seek significant relationships that are in quality like the duet of mother and unborn. The genetic code demands that we find ways to be related to others in tandem.

Consider the similarity between the plea of the Phantom to Christine and the plea of Ruth to Naomi in the Book of Ruth:

> Do not press me to leave you or to turn back from following you! Where you go, I will go; where you lodge, I will lodge; your people shall be my people, and your God my God. Where you die, I will die—there will I be buried. May the LORD do thus and so to me, and more as well, if even death parts me from you! (Ru 1:16-17)[3]

The same theme can be found all through the history of literature and art. We are hungry for someone to invite us to go a distance with them, or to respond to our invitation to go with us.

But wait, what about standing on our own two feet? What about the trap of dependency? Shouldn't we encourage independence in a world that can't be trusted? Wouldn't Ruth be diagnosed as a co-dependent, a ripe candidate to marry an alcoholic and live a miserable life and wind up the subject of a country and western song?

The story says different. It presents to us a picture of a woman who knew her need to be related, asked for it to be filled and allowed another to provide it. I like to think that it was the freely-given acceptance of her by Naomi that encouraged Ruth to get on with her life and to sing her duet with many other people before she died. Lucky for Boaz that Naomi had let her come along, for it was the yes Naomi said to Ruth that relit the hope and expectation that there would be other duets to come. Their duet was not an imprisonment; rather, it was a freedom.

Good Me, Bad Me, Not Me

Down to the vaults the Phantom carried the kidnaped Christine, with Raoul in pursuit. The Phantom captures and imprisons Raoul and delivers this ultimatum to Christine: "Stay with me or he dies. Love me or he is history." The impossibility of the deal faces Christine like a monster. If she says yes to the Phantom, she only affirms that she cares for Raoul. If she says no, Raoul dies. She must say yes and mean it. In a moment of empathy that speaks volumes about our capacity to see our own soul's struggle in another's, Christine embraces the Phantom with unmistakable compassion. She sings:

> Pitiful creature of darkness
> What kind of life have you known?
> God give me courage
> To show you
> You are not alone. . . . (act II, scene 9)[2]

And with those words, she embraces and kisses the Phantom.

Figure E.1

"THE LOOKING-GLASS SELF"

Parents or Parenting Persons

"You are lovable and capable."

"You are ugly and no good."

"You are not important enough to bother with."

"Good Me"

"Bad Me"

"Not Me"

For the briefest moment the Phantom experiences the duet life has denied him. For at that moment something healthy, noble and kind replaced the smoldering rage within. It became clear what he should do. He released both Christine and Raoul and let that brief duet be enough to remind him of his humanity.

Such is the power of the loving duet: to transform the ugly and disfigured soul into the beauty it is. It can serve as a model of part of our ministry in the world: to invite the aching soloists to sing the duets that, to quote another song, "melt our souls down to where they want to be."

A century ago Charles Cooley concluded that our self images come from the "reflection" we see of ourselves in the way others treat us. He called it the "Looking-Glass Self." If we are thought of and treated as valuable and unique by the ones who raise us, that is the way we will come to see ourselves.[4]

Fifty years later Harry Stack Sullivan (see Figure E.1) took the idea further by saying that each of us develops a self image that falls into three categories, depending on the predominant way we were treated and seen by our parents: "good me" (if we were treated with respect, love and affection), "bad me" (if we were treated with disrespect, meanness and harshness), and "not me" (if we were ignored, avoided and left out of our parents' life). Our behavior and way we look at life is directed by these three self images: "good me" affirms life and people, "bad me" strikes out at life and others, and "not me" seeks to get the attention of others in ways that tend to be self destructive.[5]

The duet has the power to reorganize one's world-model so that the present and future look hopeful or dismal. When someone takes the risk of entering into another's life bearing love and respect for even a moment, and in spite of a wall of isolation that may have been erected, lives get transformed. There is not one of us who does not crave it, and there is not one of us who cannot offer it to another.

I invite you to find ways to join your song with that of others in work, worship, play and celebration. I invite you to find ways to assist emotionally abandoned children of every age to sing again the duet they were denied by those who raised them, and to find ways to assist spouses to rediscover the duet that can light hope again in a marriage. I invite you to find ways you can do ministry that put people together in teams and pairs, where they can share each other and enter into each other's lives as they do ministry. I invite you to look at your own life and find the courage to sing a new song with the God of love, and with your brothers and sisters.

In the final analysis, our greatest strength as educators rests on our personal presence as a friend. Friends together help each other build the models of the world, acquire the knowledge and learn the skills that reconnect us with what is at the heart of things. Friends together find ways to express the manifestos each of us seeks to make real. Let us use the power of friendship to nurture other selves in their growing awareness of self, community, creation and that which is at the core of reality.

Notes

Notes for Chapter 1

1. R. Thompson, *The Brain: An Introduction to Neuroscience* (San Francisco: W. H. Freeman & Co., 1985): 253.

2. J. Z. Young, *Programs of the Brain* (Oxford: Oxford University Press, 1978): 146.

3. K. Klivington, *The Science of Mind* (Cambridge, Massachusetts: The MIT Press, 1989): 147.

4. Young, 9.

5. I. Rock, *Perception* (New York: Scientific American Books, 1984): 83.

6. Young, 117.

7. Ibid., 120.

8. Ibid., 146.

9. J. Campbell, *Grammatical Man* (New York: Simon and Schuster, 1982): 127.

10. C. Hampden-Turner, *Maps of the Mind* (New York: Macmillan, 1981): 146.

11. J. Anderson, *Cognitive Psychology and Its Implications* (San Francisco: W. H. Freeman & Co., 1986): 32.

12. C. Furst, *The Origins of the Mind* (Englewood Cliffs, New Jersey: Prentice-Hall, 1979): 45-46.

13. Ibid., 28.

14. J. Fincher, *The Brain: Mystery of Matter and Mind* (New York: Torstar Books, 1984): 22.

15. Ibid., 122.

16. G. R. Taylor, *The Natural History of the Mind* (New York: Dutton, 1979): 29.

17. Thompson, 24.

18. Furst, 39.

19. Taylor, 154.

20. Furst, 189-90.

21. Klivington, 195.

22. S. Springer & G. Deutsch, *Left Brain, Right Brain,* Third ed. (San Francisco: W. H. Freeman & Co., 1989): 67.

23. Klivington, 135.

24. G. Miller, *The Science of Words* (New York: Scientific American Library, 1991): 96.

25. Ibid., 174.

26. Springer & Deutsch, 284.

Notes for Chapter Two

1. J. B. Hellige, *Hemispheric Asymmetry* (Cambridge, Massachusetts: Harvard University Press, 1993): 40.

2. Ibid., 35.

3. H. Gardner, *Multiple Intelligences* (New York: Basic Books, 1993): 5.

4. M. Hunt, *The Universe Within* (New York: Simon and Schuster, 1982).

5. J. P. Frisby, *Seeing* (New York: Oxford University Press, 1980): 39.

6. J. Anderson, *Cognitive Psychology and its Implications* (San Francisco: W. H. Freeman & Co., 1986): 128.

7. G. R. Taylor, *The Natural History of the Mind* (New York: Dutton, 1979): 114.

8. E. Erikson, *Childhood and Society* (New York: W. W. Norton & Co., 1963): 261-63.

9. J. B. Salinger, The *Catcher in the Rye* (New York: Bantam Books, 1951): 197-98.

10. A. Baddeley, *Your Memory: A User's Guide* (New York: Macmillan, 1982): 12.

11. Ibid., 13.

12. D. C. Dennett, *Consciousness Explained* (Boston: Little, Brown & Co., 1991): 416.

Notes for Chapter Three

1. J. A. Simpson and E. S. C. Weiner, eds., *The Compact Oxford English Dictionary*, 2nd ed. (Oxford: Clarendon Press, 1991): 496.

2. Ibid., 1552.

3. Ibid., 1189.

4. T. Kagawa, *Meditations* (New York: Harper & Brothers, 1959): 22.

5. *The Compact Oxford English Dictionary*, 2093.

6. M. Snyder, R. Snyder, & R. Snyder Jr., *The Young Child As Person* (New York: Human Sciences Press, 1980): 13-14.

7. *The Compact Oxford English Dictionary*, 1420.

8. Ibid., 846.

9. *The Interpreter's Dictionary of the Bible*, vol. 2 (Nashville: Abingdon Press, 1962): 605.

10. *The Compact Oxford English Dictionary*, 527.

11. M. L'Engle, *Everyday Prayers*, (New York: Morehouse-Barlow, 1974): 207.

12. *The Compact Oxford English Dictionary*, 2016.

13. L. Fisher, *Gandhi* (New York: New American Library, 1954).

14. J. Campbell, *The Hero with a Thousand Faces* (New Jersey: Princeton University Press, 1949).

15. Snyder, Snyder & Snyder, 218.

Notes for Chapter Four

1. M. Hunt, *The Universe Within* (New York: Simon and Schuster, 1982): 17-46.

2. Hunt, 157-95.

3. C. Rogers, *Counseling and Psychotherapy* (Boston: Houghton Mifflin Co., 1942).

4. G. Thomas, *Parent Effectiveness Training* (New York: Signet, 1975).

5. J. Anderson, *Cognitive Psychology and Its Implications* (San Francisco: W. H. Freeman & Co., 1986): 128-32.

6. L. Carroll, *Alice In Wonderland* and *Through the Looking Glass* (New York: J. M. Dent, 1993): 166.

Notes for Chapter Five

1. G. Snyder, *Maps of the Heavens* (New York: Abbeville Press, 1984): 98.

2. G. M. Sesti, *The Glorious Constellations* (New York: Harry N. Abrams, Inc., Publishers, 1991): 391.

3. J. P. Frisby, *Seeing* (New York: Oxford University Press, 1980): 39.

4. I. Rock, *Perception* (New York: Scientific American Books, 1984): 11.

5. Igor Stravinsky, *Greeting Prelude,* Columbia Symphony Orchestra, #SMK 46296.

6. Frisby, 111.

7. Ibid.

8. Ibid.

9. Ibid.

10. Ibid., 114.

11. J. L. Locher, *The World of M. C. Escher* (New York: Harry N. Abrams, Inc., 1971): 143.

12. J. Block & H. Yuker, *Can You Believe Your Eyes?* (New York: Garden Press, Inc., 1989): 37.

13. Frisby, 111.

14. H. Keller, *The World I Live In* (New York: Century Co., 1908): 27.

Notes for Chapter Six

1. J. Westerhoff III, *Will Our Children Have Faith?* (San Francisco: Harper & Row Publishers, Inc., 1976): 51-78.

2. J. Wach, *The Comparative Study of Religions* (New York, Columbia University Press, 1958): 30-37.

3. P. Tillich, *The Courage To Be* (New Haven: Yale University Press, 1952): 47.

4. H. Cox, *The Seduction of the Spirit* (New York: Simon and Schuster, 1973): 15-19.

Notes for Chapter Seven

1. J. Jaynes, *The Origins of Consciousness in the Breakdown of the Bicameral Mind* (Boston: Houghton Mifflin Company, 1976): 52-56.

2. M. Hunt, *The Universe Within* (New York: Simon and Schuster, 1982): 292.

3. C. Funk, *A Hog on Ice* (New York: Harper Colophon Books, 1985): 168.

4. Hunt, 142.

5. R. Snyder, *The Ministry of Meaning* (Geneva, Switzerland: Youth Department of the World Council of Churches, 1965).

6. M. Samuels & N. Samuels, *Seeing with the Mind's Eye* (New York: Random House, 1975): 209-36.

7. Ibid.

8. S. McFague, *Models of God* (Philadelphia: Fortress Press, 1987): 181-87.

9. Hunt, 274.

10. H. Gardner, *Creating Minds* (New York: Basic Books, 1993): 104.

11. Hunt, 291.

12. J. L. Phillips, *The Origins of Intellect: Piaget's Theory* (San Francisco: W. H. Freeman & Co., 1969): 26-51.

13. J. Anderson, *Cognitive Psychology and Its Implications* (San Francisco: W. H. Freeman & Co., 1986): 69.

14. C. Hampden-Turner, *Maps of the Mind* (New York: Macmillan, 1981): 102.

Notes for Chapter Eight

1. M. McLuhan, *Understanding Media: The Extensions of Man* (New York: McGraw-Hill, 1964).

2. M. Hunt, *The Universe Within* (New York: Simon and Schuster, 1982): 101-12.

3. S. Kosslyn & M. Koenig, *Wet Mind* (New York: Free Press, 1992): 387.

4. A. Baddeley, *Your Memory: A User's Guide* (New York: Macmillan, 1992): 169-87.

5. Ibid., 119-22.

6. Ibid., 152-54.

7. J. Kotre, *White Gloves* (New York: The Free Press, 1995): 59-84.

8. Baddeley, 75.

9. Ibid., 83.

10. Ibid., 15-17.

11. Kosslyn & Koenig, 56-57.

12. Ibid., 380-86.

13. J. Anderson, *Cognitive Psychology and Its Implications* (San Francisco: W. H. Freeman & Co., 1986): 149-54.

14. S. Rose, *The Making of Memory* (New York: Anchor Books, 1992): 117-21.

Notes for Chapter Nine

1. R. Snyder. *Ministry of Meanings* (Geneva, Switzerland: Youth Department of the World Council of Churches, 1965).

2. S. Kierkegaard, *Either/Or* (Garden City, N.Y.: Doubleday, 1959).

3. T. Groome, *Christian Religious Education* (San Francisco: Harper & Row, 1980): 152-77.

Notes for Chapter Ten

1. H. Gardner, *Frames of Mind* (New York: Basic Books, 1983).

2. Ibid., 62.

3. H. Gardner, *Multiple Intelligences* (New York: Basic Books, 1993): 21.

4. Ibid., 21.

5. Ibid., 17.

6. Ibid., 19.

7. Ibid., 18.

8. Ibid., 22.

9. Ibid., 24.

10. H. Gardner, *The Mind's New Science* (New York: Basic Books, 1985): 71.

11. S. Springer & G. Deutsch, *Left Brain, Right Brain* (San Francisco: W. H. Freeman & Co.): 27-71.

12. C. Furst, *The Origins of the Mind* (Englewood Cliffs, New Jersey: Prentice-Hall): 149-53.

13. S. Springer & G. Deutsch, 296-300.

Notes for Chapter Eleven

1. P. Tillich, *The Eternal Now* (New York: Charles Scribner's Sons, 1963): 122.

2. H. Potthoff, *The Inner Life* (Nashville: Graded Press, 1969): 66.

3. J. Campbell, *The Hero with a Thousand Faces* (New Jersey: Princeton University Press, 1949): 46.

4. Ibid., 46.

5. Ibid., 122.

6. Ibid., 217.

7. A. Prochiantz, *How the Brain Evolved* (New York: McGraw-Hill, 1989): 74-80.

8. E. Erikson, *Childhood and Society* (New York: W. W. Norton & Company, 1963).

9. J. Phillips, *The Origins of Intellect: Piaget's Theory* (New York: Harper & Row, 1982).

10. M. Wilcox, *Developmental Journey* (Nashville: Abingdon Press, 1979).

11. J. Fowler, *Stages of Faith* (Cambridge: Harper & Row, 1881).

12. C. E. Nelson, ed., *Congregations, Their Power to Form and Transform* (Atlanta: John Knox Press, 1988).

13. Ross Snyder, *Young People and Their Culture* (Nashville: Abingdon Press, 1969).

14. Paul Irwin, *The Care and Counseling of Youth in the Church* (Philadelphia: Fortress Press, 1975).

15. M. Snyder, R. Snyder & R. Snyder Jr., *The Young Child as Person* (New York: Human Sciences Press, 1980): 217.

16. M. Buber, *I and Thou* (New York: Charles Scribner's Sons, 1958): 11.

Notes for Chapter Twelve

1. E. Erikson, *Childhood and Society* (New York: W. W. Norton and Co., 1963): 261.

2. R. Winn, *A Concise Dictionary of Existentialism* (New York: Book Sales, Inc., 1960): 22.

3. H. Thoreau, *Walden* (New York: Washington Square Press, 1963): 66.

4. A. Schutz, *Collected Papers I* (The Hague, Netherlands: Martinus Nijhoff, 1964): 213.

5. D. Dennett, *Consciousness Explained* (Boston: Little, Brown and Co., 1991): 21-25.

6. R. Ornstein, *The Evolution of Consciousness* (New York: Prentice Hall Press, 1991): 34-39.

7. G. Taylor, *The Natural History of the Mind* (New York: Dutton, 1979): 187.

8. Dennett, 364-66.

9. Ornstein, 208-14.

10. Dennett, 368.

11. Ibid., 240-41.

12. Ibid., 181.

13. Ibid.

14. Ibid., 49.

15. Ibid., 194-99.

16. J. Jaynes, *The Origin of Consciousness in the Breakdown of the Bicameral Mind* (Boston: Houghton Mifflin Company, 1976): 204-15.

17. Ibid., 214.

18. H. Keller, *The World I Live In* (New York: Century Co., 1908).

19. E. Hearth, *The Creative Loop* (Reading, Massachusetts: Addison-Wesley Publishing Co., 1995): 134-48.

20. Jaynes, 1-18.

21. Ibid, 219.

22. Ibid., 59-66.

23. Taylor, 248.

24. This is the concept behind Bernard Baars's book, *In the Theater of Consciousness: The Work Space of the Mind* (New York: Oxford University Press, 1997).

25. R. Coles, *The Call of Stories* (Boston: Houghton Mifflin Company, 1989): 7.

26. D. Miller, *Story and Context* (Nashville: Abingdon Press, 1987): 117-18.

27. J. Neihardt, *Black Elk Speaks* (London: University of Nebraska Press, 1961).

28. M. Greene, *Landscapes of Learning* (New York: Teachers College Press, 1978): 42-51.

29. Neihardt, 5-6.

Notes for the Epilogue

1. A. Schutz, *Collected Papers II* (The Hague, Netherlands: Martinus Nijhoff, 1964).

2. C. Hart & R. Stilgoe, *The Phantom of the Opera* (London: The Really Useful Group P.L.C., 1986).

3. Division of Christian Education, National Council of Churches of Christ in the United States, *The New Revised Standard Version Bible*, 1989.

4. C. Cooley, *Human Nature and the Social Order* (New York: Charles Scribner's Sons, 1902).

5. H. Sullivan, *Conceptions in Modern Psychiatry* (New York: Norton, 1953)

Bibliography

Anderson, John, *Cognitive Psychology and its Implications*. San Francisco: W.H. Freeman & Co., 1986.

———, *The Architecture of Cognition*. Boston, Massachusetts: Harvard University Press, 1983.

Arnheim, Rudolf, *Visual Thinking*. Berkeley: University of California Press, 1969.

Baddeley, Alan, *Your Memory: A User's Guide*. New York: Macmillan, 1982.

Baars, Bernard J., *In the Theater of Consciousness—The Workspace of the Mind*. New York: Oxford University Press, 1997.

Block, J. Richard, Harold Yuker, *Can You Believe Your Eyes?* New York: Gardner Press, Inc., 1989.

Bloom, Floyd E., & Lazerson, Arlyne, *Brain, Mind and Behavior*. New York: W. H. Freeman & Co., 1985.

Brodal, Per, *The Central Nervous System*. New York: Oxford University Press, 1992.

Buber, Martin, *I and Thou*. New York: Charles Scribner's Sons, 1958.

Buttrick, George, ed., *Interpreter's Dictionary of the Bible*. Nashville: Abingdon Press, 1962.

Buzan, Tony, *Use Both Sides of your Brain*. New York: E. P. Dutton, 1983.

Calvin, William H., George A. Ojemann, *Conversations With Neil's Brain*. Reading, Massachusetts: Addison-Wesley, 1994.

Campbell, Jeremy, *Grammatical Man*. New York: Simon and Schuster, 1982.

Campbell, Joseph, *The Hero with a Thousand Faces*. New Jersey: Princeton University Press, 1949.

Changeux, Jean-Pierre, *Neuronal Man—The Biology of Mind*. New York: Pantheon Books,1985.

Coles, Robert, *The Call of Stories*. Boston: Houghton Mifflin Company, 1989.

———, *Erik H. Erikson, The Growth of His Work*. Boston: Little, Brown & Company, 1970.

Cooley, C. H., *Human Nature and the Social Order*. New York: Charles Scribner's Sons, 1902.

Cox, Harvey, *The Seduction of the Spirit*. New York: Simon and Schuster, 1973.

184

Damasio, Antonio R., *Descartes' Error*. New York: G. P. Putnam's Sons, 1994.

Darwin, Bernard, ed., *The Oxford Dictionary of Quotations*. New York: Oxford University Press, 1954.

Dennett, Daniel C., *Consciousness Explained*. Boston: Little, Brown and Company, 1991.

Edelman, Gerald M., *Bright Air, Brilliant Fire*. New York: Basic Books, 1992.

Erikson, Erik H., *Childhood and Society*. New York: W. W. Norton & Company, 1963.

Fincher, Jack, *The Brain: Mystery of Matter and Mind*. New York: Torstar Books, 1984.

Fischer, Louis, *Gandhi*. New York: New American Library, 1954.

Fowler, James W., *Stages of Faith*. Cambridge: Harper & Row Publishers, 1981.

Frisby, John P., *Seeing*. New York: Oxford University Press, 1980.

Funk, Charles E., *A Hog on Ice*. New York: Harper Colophon Books, 1948.

Furst, Charles, *The Origins of the Mind*. Englewood Cliffs, New Jersey: Prentice-Hall, 1979.

Gardner, Howard, *Art, Mind and Brain*. New York: Basic Books, 1982.

———, *Creating Minds*. New York: Basic Books, 1993.

———, *Frames of Mind*. New York: Basic Books, 1983.

———, *The Mind's New Science*. New York: Basic Books, 1985.

———, *Multiple Intelligences*. New York: Basic Books, 1993.

———, *The Unschooled Mind*. New York: Basic Books, 1991.

Gazzaniga, Michael S., ed., *The Cognitive Neurosciences*. Boston, Massachusetts: The MIT Press, 1995.

———, *The Social Brain*. New York: Basic Books, 1985.

Greene, Maxine, *Landscapes of Learning*. New York: Teachers College Press, 1978.

Gregory, R. L., *Eye and Brain*. New York: McGraw-Hill Book Company, 1966.

Groome, Thomas, *Christian Religious Education*. San Francisco: Harper & Row, 1980.

Hampden-Turner, Charles, *Maps of the Mind*. New York: Macmillan, 1981.

Hearth, Erich, *The Creative Loop*. Reading, Massachusetts: Addison-Wesley Publishing Company, 1993.

Hellige, Joseph B., *Hemispheric Asymmetry*. Boston: Harvard University Press, 1993.

Hofstadter, Douglas R., *Godel, Escher, Bach: An Eternal Golden Braid*. New York: Vintage Books, 1979.

————, & Daniel C. Dennett, *The Mind's I*. New York: Bantam Books, 1981.

Hunt, Morton, *The Universe Within*. New York: Simon and Schuster, 1982.

Irwin, Paul, *The Care and Counseling of Youth in the Church*. Philadelphia: Fortress Press, 1975.

Jastrow, Robert, *The Enchanted Loom: Mind in the Universe*. New York: Simon and Schuster, 1981.

Jaynes, Julian, *The Origin of Consciousness in the Breakdown of the Bicameral Mind*. Boston: Houghton Mifflin, 1976.

Johnson, George, *In the Palaces of Memory*. New York: Alfred A. Knopf, 1991.

Kagawa, Toyohiko, *Meditations*. New York: Harper & Brothers, 1950.

Keller, Hellen, *The World I Live In*. New York: Century Co., 1908.

Klivington, Kenneth, *The Science of Mind*. Boston: MIT Press, 1989.

Kosslyn, Stephen M., *Image and Brain*. Cambridge, Massachusetts: MIT Press, 1994.

————& Oliver Koenig, *Wet Mind*. New York: The Free Press, 1992.

Kotre, John, *White Gloves*. New York: The Free Press, 1995.

LeVay, Simon, *The Sexual Brain*. Boston: MIT Press, 1993.

Locher, J. L., ed., *The World of M. C. Escher*. New York: Harry Abrams Inc., 1971.

Marr, David, *Vision*. San Francisco: W. H. Freeman & Co., 1982.

McFague, Sallie, *Models of God*. Philadelphia: Fortress Press, 1987.

McLuhan, Marshall, *Understanding Media*. New York: New American Library, 1964.

Miller, Donald E., *Story and Context*. Nashville: Abingdon Press, 1987.

Miller, George, *The Science of Words*. New York: Scientific American Library, 1991.

Minsky, Marvin, *The Society of Mind*. New York: Simon and Schuster, 1985.

Neihardt, John G., *Black Elk Speaks*. London: University of Nebraska Press, 1961.

Nelson, C. Ellis, ed., *Congregations, Their Power to Form and Transform*. Atlanta: John Knox Press, 1988.

Nicholls, John G., Robert A. Martin & Bruce G. Wallace, *From Neuron to Brain*. Boston: Sinauer Associates, 1992.

Ornstein, Robert, *The Evolution of Consciousness*. New York: Prentice-Hall Press, 1991.

————, *The Roots of the Self*. New York: HarperSanFrancisco: 1993.

Pfeiffer, John E., *The Creative Explosion*. New York: Harper & Row, 1982.

Phillips, John L., *The Origins of Intellect: Piaget's Theory*. San Francisco: W. H. Freeman & Co., 1969.

Potthoff, Harvey, *The Inner Life*. Nashville: Graded Press, 1969.

Prochiantz, Alain, *How The Brain Evolved*. New York: McGraw-Hill Inc., 1989.

Ratner, Leonard G., *The Musical Experience*. New York: W. H. Freeman and Co., 1983.

Restak, Richard, *The Brain*. New York: Bantam Books, 1984.

———, *The Modular Brain*. New York: Lisa Drew Books, 1994.

Rivlin, Robert, & Karen Gravelle, *Deciphering the Senses*. New York: Simon and Schuster, 1984.

Rock, Irvin, *Perception*. New York: Scientific American Books, 1984.

Rose, Steven, *The Making of Memory*. New York: Anchor Books, 1992.

Rosenfield, Israel, *The Invention of Memory*. New York: Basic Books, 1988.

Salinger, J. D., *The Catcher in the Rye*. New York: Bantam Books, 1945.

Samuels, Mike, & Nancy Samuels, *Seeing with the Mind's Eye*. New York: Random House Bookworks, 1975.

Schutz, Alfred, *Collected Papers I*. The Hague, Netherlands: Martinus Nijhoff, 1964.

———, *Collected Papers II*. The Hague, Netherlands: Martinus Nijhoff, 1964.

Sesti, Giuseppe Maria, *The Glorious Constellations*. New York: Harry N. Abrams Inc., Publishers, 1991.

Shepard, Roger N., & Lynn A. Cooper, *Mental Images and their Transformations*. Boston: MIT Press, 1982.

Simpson, J. A. & Weiner, E. S. C., eds., *The Compact Oxford English Dictionary*. Oxford: Clarendon Press, 1991.

Smith, Anthony, *The Mind*. New York: The Viking Press, 1984.

Snyder, George Sergeant, *Maps of the Heavens*. New York: Abbeville Press, 1984.

Snyder, Martha, Ross Snyder & Ross Snyder, Jr., *The Young Child As Person*. New York: Human Sciences Press, 1980.

Snyder, Ross, *Ministry of Meaning*. Geneva, Switzerland: Youth Department of the World Council of Churches, 1965.

———, *Young People and Their Culture*. Nashville: Abingdon Press, 1969.

Springer, S., & G. Deutsch, *Left Brain, Right Brain*. San Francisco: W. H. Freeman & Co., 1989.

Sternberg, Robert J., *Human Abilities*. New York: W. H. Freeman & Co., 1985.

Storr, Anthony, *Music and the Brain*. New York: The Free Press, 1992.

Stravinsky, Igor, *Greeting Prelude*. Recorded by Stravinsky and the Columbia Symphony Orchestra, Dec. 17, 1963, Sony Classical Compact Disk #SMK 46296, 1991.

Sullivan, H. S., *Conceptions of Modern Psychiatry*. New York: Norton, 1953.

Taylor, Gordon Rattray, *The Natural History of the Brain*. New York: Dutton, 1979.

Thompson, Richard, *The Brain—An Introduction to Neuroscience*. San Francisco: W. H. Freeman & Co., 1985.

Tillich, Paul, *The Courage To Be*. New Haven: Yale University Press, 1952.

———, *The Eternal Now*. New York: Charles Scribner's Sons, 1963.

Young, J. Z., *Programs of the Brain*. Oxford: Oxford University Press, 1978.

Wach, Joachim, *The Comparative Study of Religion*. New York: Columbia University Press, 1958.

Westerhoff, John, *Will Our Children Have Faith?* San Francisco: Harper & Row, 1976.

Wilcox, Mary M., *Developmental Journey*. Nashville: Abingdon Press, 1979.

Wills, Christopher, *The Runaway Brain*. New York: Basic Books, 1993.

Winn, Ralph B., *A Concise Dictionary Of Existentialism*. New York: Book Sales Inc., 1960.

Zeki, Semir, *A Vision of the Brain*. Boston: Blackwell Scientific Publications, 1993.